A MASSAGE THERAPIST'S GUIDE
TO BUILDING A SIX-FIGURE BUSINESS
WITH FUN, FREEDOM AND PASSION

ELICIA CROOK AND JAMES CROOK

Dedication

To our most amazing children, Toby and Aniela – you light up our world and make us proud of your choices every second of every day.

Also to Kym Ivory and Terrie Crook, for Grandma's day and Nanna's day, for investing in our children since they were born and always supporting us – we are so grateful for everything you do for us and all the children in your care.

Elicia Crook

Elicia is a business coach and mentor to hundreds of other massage therapists, sharing the tactics she used to create her business success over 16 years. She remembers what it was like at the beginning to get up every day and treat only a handful of clients with gaps in between – and the sinking feeling when you look into next week's bookings and see it's going to be lean.

Luckily, Elicia was able to turn it around. She grew her massage business from where she started – working on family and friends in her lounge room – to at one point having nine staff and doing 100+ treatments per week across the team.

Through this experience (and by making many mistakes along the way) Elicia discovered what works and who she needed to be in order to run a successful massage business. Now she takes this blueprint to her clients to build more success and passion, and to drive the massage industry forward.

James Crook

James is a speaker, author and marketer who has run a boutique digital marketing agency since 2003, working with hundreds of small business clients each year. His earlier book *Digitally Enhanced* helps professionals to enhance their web presence to attract more of their ideal clients, and it became a #1 Best Seller on Amazon within five weeks of launch.

James is now a full-time business coach for massage therapists and gives clarity on all things to do with websites, Google, Facebook and everything else online. His gentle approach to training is easy to follow so every massage therapist can reap the benefits of online marketing.

Sprout Publishing
Geelong, Victoria, Australia

First published in 2018 by Sprout Publishing

A catalogue entry for this book is available from the National Library of Australia.

ISBN: 978-0-9943284-2-7

Project management and text design by Michael Hanrahan Publishing
Cover design by Peter Reardon

CONTENTS

INTRODUCTION

THE ADVENTURE AHEAD

Most therapists get into massage or myotherapy because they love people, love making a difference and honestly want to help and heal their clients. We quite often say that this is the world's most "touchy-feely" profession, because therapists spend so much time touching other people. But growing a business is *not* a touchy-feely process, nor an easy one, as you will know if you're trying it already. The type of energy and skills required to do bookkeeping, or marketing, or social media, or negotiating rent are very different to the energy and skills you use in the treatment room with a client.

Most massage courses include very little business training to help their enthusiastic students succeed once they get out into the real world, so it's not surprising that 70% of new massage businesses fail in the first three years, and at least half of those people who do survive more than three years earn less than minimum wage. The two of us – Elicia and James Crook – have made it our mission to reverse this trend, and to improve the health of the nation by empowering massage therapists to see more clients by using simple tools to grow their businesses.

Elicia is a massage therapist and ran her massage business for 16 years, starting by treating friends and family from our lounge room and growing to have a clinic with nine staff at one point doing over 100 treatments per week. Meanwhile, James was running a digital marketing agency, also with a handful of staff, creating websites, social media campaigns and doing other online marketing for small business clients across Australia. We didn't always get everything in these businesses right; in fact, we made a lot of mistakes! But we grew through these, and as we evolved we realised that many of the challenges we overcame could have been prevented altogether if we'd had the right training or guidance.

That's why we wrote *Fully Booked Without Burnout*, and that's why we travel Australia and the world coaching massage therapists how to serve with abundance, fun and freedom, and turn their passion into a rocking business.

But more about our story later...

THE KEY DIFFERENCE BETWEEN SUCCESS AND FAILURE

We want to start by focusing on the thing that makes the single biggest difference in any massage business, because one of the unique privileges we have is that we work with therapists from opposite ends of the business spectrum. We see those who struggle to get even a handful of clients each week, who are stressed, strained, and on the verge of burnout because they can't see how to make their businesses work. We also see the people who run massage businesses that turn over $500k and even $1m or more each year. And we see everything in between.

So what's the biggest difference between these extremes?

By far the biggest single distinction is this: *commitment*.

The people who become successful are relentlessly committed to the dream they want to achieve, and their level of commitment gives them a few other superpowers in common. Their commitment allows them to believe in themselves and their future enough to take action towards where they want to go. And it's action that makes things happen. It's action that leads to success. Even small actions, taken regularly, lead to a big journey being covered over time. This is the power of consistent, committed action in the one direction.

Now your ambition might not be to hit seven figures, or even six, but we bet you do want to see abundance in your business so that it can be easier and more successful, whatever that looks like for you. To make that happen you must have the endgame in mind and do what it takes to get there. If you focus on a clear goal it's like a compass pointing out the path in front of you at every step.

Yes, it will be difficult sometimes. Yes, there will be challenges. Yes, there will be uncomfortable steps that you don't want to take.

But guess what? Do it anyway! When you do, you'll discover that you grow and change and the steps that seemed so challenging before all of a sudden appear smaller. Whether you are just starting out or you are a seasoned veteran looking to move to the next stage of your business – whatever your next steps look like – sometimes getting started can be the hardest part.

THREE COMMON MYTHS AND HOW TO OVERCOME THEM

We want to share with you the three big myths we hear most often that stop people moving forward, and how you can overcome these to create a profitable business that you love.

Myth #1: If I'm a good therapist my business will grow naturally

Every business that succeeds needs certain things to happen as part of the way it works. A business is like a living tree with different parts that connect and feed off each other. For example, you need clients coming in consistently; you need to do a good job treating them so they have great outcomes, so that they come back and also tell others about you; and you as the therapist need to have your financial and lifestyle needs met so you can keep the tree alive.

The truth: If you're not planning and caring for the different parts of your tree it's like planting a sapling in your garden but never watering it, or weeding, or staking, or pruning. The tree will grow – perhaps – but it will be stumpy and spindly and slow to bear fruit.

Sometimes we do see a business that works by relying on word-of-mouth referrals and not much else, but this is a slow way to grow and it doesn't give you any control over the shape or health of your business. When difficult times come – and they always come – these business owners see their trees bend and sometimes break, and they must quickly strive to learn new skills or the tree will die.

Instead, if you proactively care for your business using the strategies we show you in this book, you'll grow a strong tree that is proud and tall and healthy, and that will withstand the challenging winds when the storms come.

Myth #2: I am "heart-centred" so I focus on my clients and not money

Some therapists strongly dislike the idea of business success, and may even feel guilty asking for payment for their services. They might say things like, "I just want to help people so much that I feel bad if they have to pay for it", or even, "I don't want to make money".

The myth here is that helping clients and running a successful business are mutually exclusive.

The truth: Building a successful business allows you to help *more* people.

What is the definition of a "successful business"? The best meaning we can think of is that a successful business allows you to positively impact the health and wellbeing of your community. This can be in a big way or a modest way depending on your ambition, but whatever size your dreams are, they can't be achieved without treating people.

It took both of us a long time to realise that when you run a heart-centred business and help people, you will make money at the same time. When you run your business from an authentic, connected, heart-centred space then everything you do will focus on helping your clients. And when you help people they will be happy to pay, which in turn allows you to pay your rent, pay yourself, pay for marketing so even more people hear about your skills... which allows you to help even more people. And the more money you have, the more you can make a difference in other ways too. You can educate and treat even more people in your community and further afield.

If we are going to raise the professional standards of massage and raise awareness of massage as a legitimate part of the health industry, we need to have a paradigm shift around this idea that money is somehow bad and that we can't make any as a therapist. Not everyone wants to focus on business skills and that's actually totally fine, but if you're one of these people our strongest advice would be to find someone who is running an awesome business already and work for them as an employee.

If you're striking out on your own then you need to take it on board with energy and take the action required to make it work. You owe it to your clients, to your community, to your family and to yourself.

Myth #3: I don't have the skills or talents to run a business like other more successful people do

It can sometimes feel overwhelming when you see others who have achieved a high level of success already. They often seem to have everything together in a way that you do not.

The truth: Everyone who is ahead of you in any way is there only because they've learned some things they needed to learn and have then consistently taken the required steps to get where they want to go. It might look easy for them now because they have momentum and a good reputation, but everyone starts from the same place, and even the most successful people have had to learn what they need to do in order to get there.

Any new task at the start looks difficult; it's like climbing a mountain and being daunted as you stand at the bottom looking up. But when you keep taking small steps towards your end goal you discover the skills you need as you go. Every new experience makes it easier to overcome the next challenge and take the next step. Until, voilà! You've made the climb too, and you're on top of the mountain running a thriving business, even though it seemed so overwhelming at the beginning.

The fact that you've got this book in your hands shows you're willing to learn and you're ready for action. Well done! Even if you don't have some of the required skills right now, you have begun the climb and you're ready to take action and make a difference to your business.

CHAMPION SNAPSHOT: MELISSA LATU

Melissa is a single mum who has been a massage therapist for many years but only did one or two treatments each week and worked another job. It was a big decision for her to start working with us as she committed to taking her business from being a hobby to something more serious. One of her major breakthroughs was mindset: previously she had told herself that she couldn't run a successful business and also be a great mum. Once she realised that she *could* do both, her energy and focus shifted so that she was able to grow her client base quickly, leave her other job and massage full time. And she's a better mum than ever for her two kids!

BECOMING A HEALTH LEADER

So how do you know what goal to set for yourself?

Across the industry there are people walking a similar journey to you, building their massage businesses as they move forward into their version of success. Some people are already ahead, some people are probably earlier on in the journey than you.

If you ask these people, you'll get dozens of different opinions about what you should do. Already we bet you've discovered that so many of these therapists have different goals and are doing different activities to grow and drive their businesses. This can be really confusing and overwhelming when you're trying to build your business – which path is right for you?

The "Health Leader Ladder"

We've created a really useful framework to cut through this noise and bring instant clarity to your situation. We call this the "Health Leader Ladder". The ladder shows the journey that every therapist must travel when they're running their own business, and the focus points that are required at each level. This is powerful because it gives context as to why different therapists often seem to have such a different attitude to where they are in business, or what steps are most important to be successful.

The most important steps for you right now depend on what stage on the ladder you are at currently and how high you want to climb. Many people who are just starting out are near the bottom and will say things like, "I would be happy to get to Rising Star level. I just want to be booked out!" – and if that's you, that's great. This is your life and your goals, so create the lifestyle that you want. Other people look further up the ladder, and whether they are right at the bottom or already halfway up, they aspire to reach the topmost rungs and be seen as industry leaders with a broad influence. That's fine too!

But even the people who want to reach the very top levels still must work through the bottom ones first. There's no way around them. This is the same for massage therapists or anyone in related health fields (or in any other industry). The lower levels allow you to master the skills and build the personal endurance required to continue the journey upward. If you try to skip a level without having learnt the lessons it teaches, you'll be top heavy and in danger of falling over.

Take a look at the ladder and you will see how it works.

The "Health Leader Ladder"

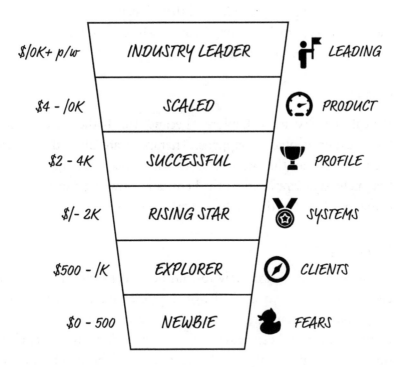

Revenue	Level		Focus
$10K+ p/w	INDUSTRY LEADER		LEADING
$4 - 10K	SCALED		PRODUCT
$2 - 4K	SUCCESSFUL		PROFILE
$1 - 2K	RISING STAR		SYSTEMS
$500 - 1K	EXPLORER		CLIENTS
$0 - 500	NEWBIE		FEARS

Newbies

When first starting out on their own, the biggest challenge for new therapists is to overcome fears. These can include:

- fear of being unsuccessful
- fear of not earning enough money
- uncertainty around their skill level
- overwhelm at all the things that need to be done if they are to move to the next step.

Through gaining experience, these newbies are able to see that a career in massage is possible, and that if they take the right action they'll be able to make it work. Fear is overcome and they will commit to making this business work.

Explorers

We call the next level "Explorer" because this is the stage where a lot of experimentation happens. Therapists are often discovering the type of client they want to work with most, what modalities or treatment styles resonate with them, and how their business will come together. The biggest focus at this level is getting more clients.

Rising Stars

Rising Stars have learnt how to gain new clients and have a good client base, and the next challenge is systemisation so that they can keep going and growing without burning out. Running a manual diary might have been easy at the lower ladder rungs but by the time they're fully booked with clients it takes too much time and effort. This pattern is repeated across the business, so a Rising Star needs to focus on how to put structures in place and outsource simple tasks so they can keep doing what they like best.

Successful

By the stage we call "Successful", a therapist has systems in place and the business is beginning to feel good. They'll be turning over a good amount, and maybe have a couple of staff on board or be starting to look at other growth pillars in their business. At this point they need to focus on raising their profile in order to sustain growth and solidify their reputation. This means introducing higher level marketing like publications, podcasts and speaking at events.

Scaled

The next step is "Scaled", and it's a very important phase for therapists who have a bigger vision, because at this stage they often need to look beyond massage or other physical treatments. To scale they must develop one or two growth pillars as sources of income that escape the direct "time for money" exchange and become more leveraged. For example, they may create group workshops, a retreat, an online program or a product line.

Industry Leaders

After successfully scaling at this level an individual can be truly classed an "Industry Leader". They'll probably be speaking at conferences, getting interviewed for magazines or podcasts, and doing regular thought-leader-style marketing. They'll still be working hard but the pillars they've already created mean that the time and energy they put in is leveraged to allow them to earn a lot more income and impact many more people.

The point to this is to show you a basic pathway of where you can go in this industry, if you choose. There is amazing opportunity for advancement. And there are also many therapists who are happy and fulfilled once they get to the "successful" stage.

The big point is that each step requires its own learning. The skills that get you through your current challenges won't be the same as the skills you need for the challenges later. Each level you achieve becomes the platform for the next stage of learning. We often joke with clients that once you overcome the challenges of the level you're on, you now get to see what the next set of challenges

11

are. You get to move to a higher class of problem to solve, and it's a never-ending pathway.

And it doesn't matter if it takes a long time, or if you can't see yourself ever wanting to reach the top rungs of the ladder. This is *your* journey, and we want to make sure you love it for life. It's also incredibly rewarding, as the challenges lead to personal and professional growth, and you get to help more and more people as you build a long-term career.

So what does success look like for *you*? How do you know where to point this compass so that you can achieve your goals? How high on the ladder do you want to climb? Let's have a look …

How many clients should you be seeing? We believe every individual therapist has an intuitive number of clients that they want to see each week; for some it's 25 or 30, while for others who might have young children or health conditions, they are happy seeing 10 to 15.

There is no right or wrong number – whatever number you focus on should be what is ideal for you. You only want to work 44 weeks each year and spend the extra time with your kids on school holidays? Rock on! Or maybe you do mobile massage and charge $120 a session? You might only need to see 12 clients a week to make it work for you. Great! What if you are already full and your dream is to have some other therapists working for you to take the load off your hands? Love it!

Why be "reasonable"?

You can reach your goals no matter what they are! We regularly see therapists achieving these inspirational milestones, and much more. But – and this is important – first you need to purposefully, powerfully and honestly set solid goals so they are a compass point in the future to guide your way forward.

What we find is that many therapists are afraid of actually putting it out there. It's like they have this feeling that if they wish for something too good, they are more likely to be disappointed. So they don't even set the goal in the first place. And if they *do* think about their ideal future at all, they push it aside and tell themselves to "be more reasonable".

More reasonable?! What a load of baloney!

Without a goal you go nowhere, just like if you're wandering in the desert without a compass. You move a little this way, a little that way, time passes, and all you've done is zigzag and make very little progress.

Downsizing your goals or shifting your focus to align with what you think other people will accept doesn't help you reach your ideal future. It may actually drive you off course. Instead, follow the direct path towards your goal, and whether your steps are fast or slow you will always be getting closer. Once you know what's possible and define what you want, all you need to do is reverse engineer that to see a pencil sketch of what the journey will look like. Then you take action, and it gets closer, and you can fill in the detail as you gain clarity and perspective. Just repeat this over and over – and over – and you'll get where you want to go.

That's where this book comes in. We'll look at setting powerful goals later.

HOW TO GET TO SIX FIGURES AS A MASSAGE THERAPIST

One question we get asked by some therapists is – what *is* "six figures"? It's a great question! $100,000 has six digits in it, and if a business has this turnover or more, we can call it a six-figure business.

And just for those who might not be familiar with the terminology:

- "turnover" is all the money that comes into your account when you do a massage and get paid for it

- "profit" is the money left over after your clients have paid you and you have paid all your bills.

So if you turn over six figures but pay for room rental, advertising, towels, oil and so on, the income in your pocket would be less all those expenses.

Now comes the maths. If you charge $90 a session, see 25 clients a week and do that 48 weeks of the year, this comes to $108,000 turnover. Remember that this is *turnover*, not *profit*. Does that matter? It depends on your goals. If you want a six-figure *turnover* then mission accomplished! If you want a six-figure *profit* you will need to turn over even more.

This is where the "growth pillars" we mentioned above come in. As you climb the Health Leader Ladder you can add other parts to your business that allow you to serve more people in new and different ways. And by the time you add in things like product sales, group workshops, hiring other therapists, renting rooms to other modalities, creating your own online program, or a bunch of other potential activities – your business can grow exponentially and you can see how easily multiple six figures of turnover can be achieved.

The big idea is that you can make decent money being a therapist, and you can do it while helping a bunch of people to feel amazing.

Sounds easy, right? Hmm. No, it's not easy ... but simple and possible? Absolutely!

Let us show you how we did it, and then how you can use the exact same principles to do this with your business too.

OUR STORY

Before we go any further, let's introduce ourselves. You might find it useful to understand our background and where we're coming from.

Elicia

Hey! This is Elicia, and I'm going to write this section of the book just from me, as I tell my story.

When I was 12 years old I stepped into an osteopath's clinic with back pain. You see, two years earlier I had dropped 200 kg of superphosphate on my left leg with a hand trolley underneath, and it had compound fractured both bones in my lower leg, which was incredibly painful and left me with a limp. I saw the osteopath, and although he fixed the limp for me, I developed back pain again some time later. I saw a different osteo for more treatment, and he mentioned scoliosis (curvature of the spine) but told me I would grow out of it.

Six months after that I was still in pain, so I was booked in to see a remedial massage therapist. She immediately saw something was wrong with my back and recommended I see a specialist. I got a referral from my GP, and six weeks later I was at the specialist, who wore a very serious expression as he looked at my x-rays with me. He told me I had severe scoliosis that would require surgery. It was indeed very severe – I still have the x-rays, and looking at them now, with the knowledge that I have, I can see how my spine was incredibly malformed. I had 32-degree curvature at the top and 27 at the bottom. From the back my spine looked like a letter "S" instead of an "I".

While I was on the waiting list for surgery I had regular massage, which relieved the physical pain I experienced. And even more than that, it helped me become more comfortable with who I

15

was in my body, as the scoliosis meant I didn't look like my friends as we entered our mid teens together.

My surgery in 1996 was successful, and I still have a metal rod and several pins in my back. James says I'm like the bionic woman. And no, I don't make the airport security alarms go off!

After this experience I found a passion to become a remedial massage therapist and run my own business, so I left high school, got a job to pay for my massage course, and went into it at age 18.

When I finished my study, I first ran my own business out of a chiropractic clinic and also worked at a day spa. I did this juggle for three years before James and I decided to go on a little life adventure and we did a season at the snow in Victoria. It was a fabulous season for snowboarding and working hard! But when I came back, the business I was running from the chiropractic clinic had come to a complete halt – all my clients had disappeared while I was gone, and I had to rebuild from scratch.

I still didn't really know what I was doing, but I came up with the idea to do a "buy one massage, get one free" special to get all my regulars back in. And it worked! Almost everyone returned. The price I paid was that I worked my second month back for free, but it was worth it to me because I knew these regulars would rebook again and again.

This experience got me thinking about what else I could do to help build my business even more, so the next month I changed the offer. This time I told all my regulars that they could give their friends a special referral deal: each regular received a voucher to give out so a friend could buy one massage and get a second massage at half price.

This went even better than I expected: when their friends came in for their second treatment, many of them rebooked and became regulars as well. I then gave them each the same vouchers for their

16

friends. This single campaign doubled my business in a matter of a few weeks.

I worked from the chiro clinic for another 12 months, building consistently, before I went completely out on my own and rented my own room. It wasn't long before I needed to hire. I found someone, but I wasn't a great leader at the time and after 12 months the poor guy only had one regular client. I'd been getting new clients through the door but didn't understand how to encourage and train my staff member to rebook the clients he was seeing.

He and I parted ways, and I became more focused on hiring and training. It took about another 12 months, and I then had five contractors working various shifts from that one treatment room. We all did crazy hours so that we could share the space, and it worked for a while, but it started to feel ridiculous when several of us wanted to fit more shifts in. So we expanded again, this time to a commercial clinic nearby. This move tripled our space and more than tripled our rent, but this clinic had the potential to be the dream business I'd always wanted. I spent the next five years learning everything I needed to know to grow and run an amazing business.

At one point we employed seven therapists, two admin staff, we saw over 100 clients per week, and we rented space to an osteopath, naturopath and life coach as well. We were the most expensive clinic on the peninsula, and there were about 30 other massage therapists in our town of Ocean Grove at the time.

Looking back at the entire 16-year journey of running that clinic, I have to say that it was one of the most powerful, engaging and formative experiences of my life. I loved going to work, my team were fantastic, we enjoyed beautiful support from our clients, and I was well known within the local community (which, I'm not going to lie, I loved!). There were also times I had to overcome massive challenges, which stretched me to tears. Sometimes the decisions I had to make tore at my heart, but even those were steps of maturity and growth.

One incredibly difficult time was when we transitioned from independent contractors to employees when the regulations changed. We realised that we had to change to an employee arrangement even though all our contractors were happy with the written agreements we had. When we transitioned across, we lost five of our team in three weeks. This disaster dropped our capacity from 100-plus treatments to about 30, and brought massive financial difficulties. Plus we were right in the middle of building our first home so we were paying rent at the same time as a mortgage – not a good time for the business to struggle.

It was also our daughter's kinder year and I wanted to be home more with the kids. But instead I found myself working in the clinic more than ever before, to keep it running as I scrambled to build the team again. Over the next eight weeks I hired five new therapists and two admin staff. It took us some three months to get the marketing right, get the systems ironed out, and train the team up before we were fully booked again.

This was by far the most challenging time of my life, and to this day I am still not sure how I found the depth of commitment I needed. But with support from my family, friends, and amazing new team, we got there.

As it turns out this experience was just another challenging step in the business, and I learnt an incredible amount from it that meant I was a better leader afterward. Along with everything else in my business it has shaped my life and has made me the person I am today – all while helping the lives of hundreds, or even thousands, of clients each year. I wouldn't change it for the world!

James

Hey there! This is James, and I'll tell my story here so that you can get a feel for where my skills and experiences come into the picture.

I have always loved communication and writing, so I went to uni straight from high school and completed a journalism degree. It was in the 1990s and newspapers were all moving online, and I actually found that part of it more interesting than the journalism itself – so a couple of years after graduating I went back and studied Electronic Design and Interactive Media.

I began doing website design as a freelancer while I was completing this course. At the time, the web was still fairly young (this was well before WordPress or Facebook), so every small business that wanted to be on the web had to get a web designer to help them.

For me this was an opportunity made in heaven! I got to use my graphic skills plus writing and communication, to create great websites for small business clients.

I did this for several years as a solo freelancer as I built my tech skills. Then I took the step of employing staff, and grew a small, very talented, creative team. We worked with hundreds of clients each year, from small local businesses right through to large corporations like Godfrey Hirst and Deakin University.

During this time of building websites and working with internet technology we experienced the quantum shift that the "communication revolution" had on how our clients connected with their audiences. This was the time when "smart" phones became popular and social media began to dominate communication. It's impossible to describe the difference this made to how people connect with each other. Almost every person in our society now walks around with a smartphone in their pocket that lets them talk to basically anyone else on Earth, and access any information they want, on any topic. The majority of people have their phone within arm's reach all day, and many even have it charging on their bedside table at night.

This was (and still is) a huge opportunity for businesses, and because I ran my agency I was in a unique position to see how people used it. I could see what worked and what didn't, and I was able to experiment across different strategies and compare.

In 2015 I published my first book for small business owners, sharing the marketing strategies I'd discovered in my 12 years in the industry up to that point, and I was excited to see it became an Amazon #1 bestseller in its category within six weeks of launch.

I don't mind sharing that over the years I also did a lot of experimentation with the online marketing for Elicia's clinic! Not everything worked, but we tried different things and plenty of it stuck, and we would get many new client bookings every week just from online activities.

And yes, as Elicia shared, there were a lot of challenges in the business.

There were several times when we urgently needed to grow the number of clients we had. Each time we took a bunch of reactive steps as well as relying heavily on the proactive steps we had taken over the years previous – all of which we are sharing with you in this book!

We have taken everything we both learnt from our experiences, our mentors, our training, our peers and through sheer hard work, and we now coach other therapists how to travel the same journey more easily, powerfully and quickly than we did.

What we both found is that this is a way for us to impact even more people, because when we help to grow a therapist's client base it means even more people are receiving the amazing benefits of massage or related therapies for their physical and emotional wellbeing.

In fact, we love helping therapists so much that we sold both our previous businesses so we could focus on this. We now run Massage Champions together full time, and with the help and support of our amazing family we are on a new journey helping therapists just like you to turn your passion into a rocking business.

CHAPTER 1

THE THREE AMAZING Ms

As we sat down to write this book we looked at our own experiences in business and the work we have done with hundreds of other therapists each year – and we found a surprising thing.

It turns out that all the tools, strategies and motivations that we use, to show massage therapists how to be more successful in business and build up to "Health Leader" status, can be broken down into three distinct categories, each as vital as the other two.

These are so important that we call them "The Three Amazing Ms".

They are: **Mindset, Marketing** and **Mechanics.**

If you get all of these Three Amazing Ms right in your business, you are guaranteed success. If even one of them is missing, it's like having a wheel with a flat side – it makes it very difficult to get moving, and if you do the journey is mighty bumpy.

Let's have a look at The Three Amazing Ms.

AMAZING MINDSET

Your mindset is what we call the way you think and feel about yourself and your business. It includes your motivation, your ability to direct your own action, and the self-care and balance you bring to your life.

You must have a bulletproof mindset so you can tackle the challenges that come up in business and continue moving forward. You must also take care of yourself and your soul so you have the energy to thrive in all aspects of your life. Without a good mindset you'll find yourself procrastinating, feeling overwhelmed or even going into complete burnout.

When your mindset is strong you'll have the ability to focus and to flow so that you feel perfectly balanced as you harmoniously work on the other two Ms in your business.

AMAZING MARKETING

Marketing is the most important part of growing any massage business, and when we talk about this we're really looking at any and all activity you do that has any communication with clients.

So yes, Facebook and Google are marketing. So are newspaper adverts and flyers.

But a whole host of other things come into play here as well, and give your clients an invaluable connection to who you are and what you do (and who you do it for). Things like your logo, colours, fonts, the words you use, photos you choose, even the interior design of your space (if you have one) and how you greet clients… these are all part of marketing. So is anything that grows your reputation or profile in your community, like blogging, getting referrals, attending markets or speaking at local events.

As your business grows and changes, your marketing will need to change too so that it can support your growth by continuing to attract new clients at the rate needed. This is exciting because it means your marketing tactics will change and adapt, making it a creative and authentic expression of who you are at any time.

If you rely on poor or passive marketing your business will grow slowly, if at all.

When you become proactive in your marketing you gain the skills and experience needed to attract your ideal clients and grow your business like clockwork.

AMAZING MECHANICS

This is what we call the back-end systems that make your business run smoothly and efficiently. A business with good mechanics runs like a machine, all parts connecting together well to give clients a consistent, frictionless experience.

Simple mechanics includes things like booking software, credit card payment systems and always having clean laundry for each client. As you get more advanced and move up the ladder, the mechanics grow to include hiring staff, renting rooms, staying compliant, and perhaps the delivery of additional services like classes, workshops, products or online programs.

If your business has poor mechanics it will feel unorganised and like it uses up all of your time, plus your clients may feel confused and have an inconsistent experience.

If your business has good mechanics, your clients will have an awesome experience every time, you'll be leveraging your time, and your business will have much more potential for growth.

The Three Amazing Ms

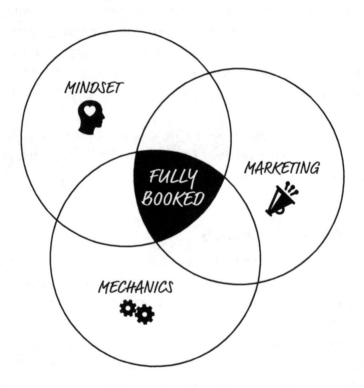

The great thing about seeing the Three Ms as a diagram like this is you can see how important each part is, and what would happen if your business wasn't balanced in all three aspects. If you have Marketing and Mechanics but miss out on having a bulletproof Mindset… you'll have plenty of clients and good systemisation, but you'll be stressed all the time and you'll feel overwhelmed to the point of burnout.

If you have Mindset and Marketing but no Mechanics... you'll be proactively attracting new clients but they'll often leave after only one or two treatments and you'll find things are constantly falling through the cracks.

And if you have Mindset and Mechanics but no Marketing... you'll be feeling good about your well-organised business, but you'll struggle to get enough clients to make ends meet.

So let's get started with the first of the Three Ms as we begin the journey to creating a truly rocking massage business!

PART I

AMAZING MINDSET

CHAPTER 2

YOUR MOST IMPORTANT TOOL FOR SUCCESS

We are starting this book with the same topic we start our programs with: **Mindset**.

There's a reason we do this. A strong mindset empowers you to stay motivated and to keep taking action along your path to reach your goals. Your mindset enables you to take action, and it's the action you take that moves you up the ladder. Your mindset also creates balance and harmony across the various aspects of your life so that you have a beautiful, centred experience every day that energises you to continue.

One of the most powerful mindset rules that successful business owners follow is the secret to living a life of fulfilment and authenticity, and also creating a business that does exactly what you want it to do.

The secret is this: every one of us creates the world we live in.

What do we mean by that?

YOUR STORY

Each of us has a story that we tell ourselves about what is happening in the world around us at any given moment. As we experience an external event through our senses, our mind will carry on a monologue that interprets the event into something that has meaning to us internally.

This is why the same event may happen to two different people and they respond in totally different ways. A man holds a door open for two women and one of them thinks "what a gentleman" while the other thinks "what a chauvinist". The experiences each woman has had in her past will create the story she tells herself about what is happening, and the meaning that each of the women gives the event is what creates their perception of the scene and the man in it.

Or have you ever been in a situation where you thought there was something going on, but a friend of yours gives you a different perspective? Maybe someone cut you off in traffic and you got mad, but your friend laughed it off because they interpret mistakes on the road differently to you.

These are simple examples of how we bring our own belief or perceptions into every situation every day, and this creates our daily experience of life.

The important thing to notice is that the physical event has no meaning until the mind interprets it. And because we live inside our own mind, we experience the interpretation, not the event itself.

Now if this is all starting to sound a bit "woo-woo" to you, just hear us out for a bit, because this idea does hold a really powerful key to living a successful life. Once you accept that the meaning of any event is interpreted by your mind, you can begin to change your mind to interpret things in the most beneficial way. This helps you maintain focus, stay motivated, and ultimately to simply enjoy your experience of the world every day.

It also explains why so many people have access to the same resources but live completely different lives. If you have an internal story that tells you you're not good enough, or this will never work, or gives you one of a million other excuses about why the events around you mean you shouldn't bother using energy to make change happen... well, the outcome is that you don't take action so the story comes true.

As coaches, we hear these stories all the time from the people we speak with, and to be truly honest we catch ourselves using them sometimes too because this is such a deeply ingrained part of the culture in our country. The stories we hear from therapists will often start with, "I've got no clients because...", and continue with things like, "my association blah blah", "the government", "I'm only Cert IV", "I live in a small town", "the economy", or one of a hundred other excuses.

But here's the thing: *what if none of that mattered?*

Other people tell themselves different stories and it changes their daily experience, which changes the action they take, which in turn creates different outcomes for them.

And even if the true reality is that some of the external circumstances might really be to blame, it is not empowering or beneficial to simply accept that. It is far more useful to act as though you believe your story of self-empowerment, because that gives you the ability to take charge of every situation.

We've seen amazing things happen when therapists commit themselves to creating their own futures and changing the story of their internal thoughts. They don't buy into the excuses that come with the circumstances, and instead they change their thoughts and actions. One therapist who had five cheap massage places open up nearby and almost kill his business launched one Facebook advert and completely changed the landscape of his business. Another beautiful therapist who was terrified of her numbers moved past that fear and tripled her revenue in 90 days, compared to the previous financial year. A therapist who was living in a share house on less than a welfare income found a loyal client base and now holidays overseas, rents her own apartment, and is saving a deposit for her own home.

We've seen therapists double their rebooking rate in a single week – simply by letting go of the fear of what people will think.

We've seen therapists invest in their business when their story tells them they have absolutely no money whatsoever – and they make it work because they seem to understand something that other people in that same situation do not.

Ultimately, it all comes down to mindset.

You can learn practical skills, have great marketing and planning, use the best booking software, understand your numbers and be a star on five social medial platforms, but if you don't address your mindset you will carry all those limiting beliefs with you and you won't succeed in the long run.

The ultimate power comes when you realise that you create the story that your mind gives you as the interpretation of your experiences.

And if you control the story… why not make it a good one?

Make it a happy story.

Make it a success story.

Make it a story that empowers you to take action.

"You have power over your mind, not outside events. Realize this, and you will find strength."

Marcus Aurelius

DEVELOPING A BULLETPROOF MINDSET

To run a business that helps people every week, and to overcome the challenges that come your way as you do, you need to have a bulletproof mindset. This means you need a way to control your narrative and tell yourself an empowering story so that you can solve your challenges, or work around them, and take action to move forward in one way or another.

It's this ability to change your own mental state and move forward that we call your "bulletproof mindset" – because when you have this kind of mindset it doesn't matter what is thrown at you, it will bounce right off.

Creating a mindset like this is like building a muscle. If you want to make a muscle strong you have to use it consistently. If you want to get a fit body, you know you can't just buy a gym membership and expect that alone to do it. Instead, you have to actively use the membership: go to the gym and work out a few times a week. Through practice, repetition and regular challenges your muscles become better at what they're doing and your body becomes strong and fit.

Tackling the path of most resistance

At the gym we do resistance exercises to build muscle. It's actually the same with mindset. In order to go to "mindset gym", you must move into the path of most resistance.

What does this mean?

It means tackling the things in your life that you find challenging, that you try to avoid doing, that you procrastinate around. These are ideas or thoughts that are giving you friction. These are the limitations on your current thinking, and they form a boundary around your current behaviours. So take notice next time you are

avoiding doing something again and again. This could
thing that is stopping you from moving forward in y
(and life).

When you think about it, this makes sense. The actions you've
taken so far have led you to the place you are right now. And the
actions you haven't taken yet will lead you to new places. By tackling that one thing you know you need to do but you haven't done
yet… you will overcome your own prior limitations and can move
up into the next level of challenges.

And the more you do it, the stronger the mindset muscle
becomes. Every new challenge is easier to tackle than the last,
because each time you have the experience of pushing through to
overcome a challenge it adds to your confidence and grows your
comfort zone.

INFLUENCING YOUR OWN MINDSET

So now that you can see why a bulletproof mindset is so important,
and you have learned about what growth you can experience from
strengthening your mindset abilities… the question we often get
asked is "how?"

How do you give yourself the best opportunity to make the
right decisions in the moment?

How can you be mindful of what is happening in the moment,
and back yourself to do what is difficult or new for you?

How's it working for you?

One of the quickest ways to change your mindset is to start asking
yourself this super-important question: *"How's it working for you?"*

This question often reveals the truth of a situation, and brings
your focus on the outcomes your action will achieve rather than

37

the task itself. For example, if you have a belief around Facebook that says, "I am no good at putting myself out there on video" – ask yourself the question, "How's it working for you?"

Not doing this task could be holding you back in your business. Focus on the outcome and do videos anyway! Trust us: the birds will not fall out of the sky if you make a mistake, and the sun will still come up tomorrow whatever happens. And the potential upside is far more powerful than any perceived downside, as you grow your tribe and your client base.

This is a perfect example of stepping into the path of most resistance and expanding your comfort zone to build a more powerful mindset. And it will build your business in the process.

Choosing your influencers

You may have heard it said that we are the average sum of the five people closest to us, in the way we think, behave, our finances and abilities. In life, you can't always choose family and friends. But in business you have the opportunity to choose who influences you, and this is powerful. Choose wisely.

If you are in a room of five people who are struggling massively with money… it won't take long and you will become the sixth.

If you are in a room of five really healthy people… you will become the sixth.

If you are in a room of five people who work hard to get to their goals… you will become the sixth.

If you are in a room of five millionaires… chances are you will become the sixth.

Now, imagine your five closest friends right now. There are certain things that you all laugh over, and that you love to talk about. And then there are other topics that are best avoided. Think about things like politics, religion, refugees, "the youth of today", or even being successful or positive. How these are discussed in your social group has a massive influence on your thinking.

As friends, who cares! But in business it's incredibly damaging if you surround yourself with small-minded people who will shoot you down when you try something new or risky.

Sometimes even well-meaning people who are employed in regular jobs or have failed to reach their own goals and dreams will project their own stories onto you to pull you down. And if you allow them to be close to you, you will become the average sum of their views.

Thankfully, you have a choice about who you let influence you.

Also, an important thing to remember is that as you start to become more aware of mindset, it can be really easy to become judgemental of others who are not on the same journey. Remember that everyone is doing the best they can with the resources they have at the time. Even the people who tear you down are actually often trying to help in their own way – they are just operating from their own patterns, experiences and beliefs in that moment.

But you know better!

Challenging yourself

If we are going to start to change the beliefs that are no longer working for us or serving us then we have to be willing to walk into the path of most resistance and keep showing up in this.

One way to practise this is to find something that is hard and commit to mastering it. This could be in any part of your life, not just business. By mastering anything that isn't easy you're building that mindset muscle for when the real challenges come along.

Maybe you don't like being organised or consistent, but you know that you need to in your business. So, start small. Commit to making your bed every morning for 30 days.

Maybe you're too concerned about what other people think of you. Start posting controversial viewpoints you believe in from your personal Facebook profile.

Maybe technology scares you. Ask a super-nice young person to show you how to post your own images on your business Facebook page. Then do one a day for a month.

Maybe doing Facebook "Lives" (live videos) scares you. Commit to do a Facebook Live daily for 30 days. This is a really good one because it breaks down a whole lot of preconceptions about what people think of you and how you can relate to your audience. Elicia has done over 200 Lives, and in our experience the most human ones – where she stuffed up the topic, or had no makeup, or had a red face after a run, or got muddled – are the most engaging Lives she's done to date.

In fact, Elicia did a Live about her journey into and out of postnatal depression on her personal Facebook profile. It's still the most watched, commented on and shared Live she has ever done, and it's because she is being as vulnerable as hell. As far as we know, no birds fell from the sky and the sun still came up the next day. However, we do know it's served many people who have watched it and have subsequently been able to reach out and ask for the help they need.

CHAPTER 3

LIVING FROM CAUSE

Once we create a better or more resourceful story about our lives and we are working on our bulletproof mindset, our next focus needs to be about responsibility.

When Elicia was growing up she had a friend who was as driven as her and the two of them would talk about how they didn't care what people thought of them, that they would make their own path, and no-one was going to find them whinging about their lives because they were going to create the lives they wanted!

They both left school early and set about creating the careers they wanted. They were not particularly entrepreneurial, and they didn't really have a clear plan for how to get where they wanted to go, but that didn't stop them from forging ahead. They knew that if it was going to happen, they would have to be the ones to do it.

ARE YOU REACTING OR RESPONDING?

Whenever any of us are faced with a situation, we have two options: we can "react" or "respond". To "react" is to take the immediate, easiest course of action in the moment, without thinking about the context or the outcome. Reactions are based on habits or primal instinct.

To "respond" is to look more openly at a situation and choose our path with consideration of what we want the outcome to be for ourselves and others.

Like when the man is holding the door open, a woman may "react" or "respond". Maybe she would react with anger, disgust or embarrassment. Or she may respond with a "thank you". The woman is not responsible for the person holding the door open, but she is responsible for how she responds to it.

The more you make a conscious choice to respond to the situations around you and be responsible for your behaviour, the more control you have. We call this responsibility "living from cause", because we put ourselves in the "cause" part of the "cause and effect" rule.

On the other hand, people who blame others for their situation and react unthinkingly are living from "effect". This is incredibly disempowering as it gives those people no control over the events of their own life.

TAKING ACTION

Living from cause gives the ability to take action and have an effect on the ultimate outcome. Let's take Jason for example, the man we mentioned earlier who had five cheaper massage places open nearby within six weeks.

Jason could have chosen to react: to get angry, frustrated, and blame the circumstances around him for not being able to grow his business. And to be fair, we're sure he had moments he felt like that. We all would.

But instead of living in that place, Jason reached out and asked for help. He accepted responsibility for what he chose to be responsible for: providing for his family, paying his rent, and running a successful business. Coming from cause allowed him to take some quick action by creating a simple Facebook advert. He spent $10 on it and got five bookings in 48 hours.

Jason kept at it, and now runs a very successful business helping heaps of people week in and week out... because he chose to come from cause and be responsible.

Another time we have seen fantastic "from cause" behaviour was with Grace, a young therapist who broke her ankle while hiking in Tasmania. Grace had every reason in the world to sit in blame, to be a victim to her circumstances, and to think it was all over as she couldn't work for 12 weeks as she recovered, and she did not have staff to cover for her.

But instead of coming from effect, Grace chose a more empowering path.

She hired a staff member from her hospital bed. She took massive action on her laptop and got her admin person to onboard the new therapist using the procedures Grace had already created. Six months later Grace had more than quadrupled her monthly business revenue. She is seeing massive success because she consistently steps up and works on her internal growth and her mindset is bulletproof.

43

DEALING WITH DISASTER

For the two of us the concept of living from cause has become a central belief that we try to live by in every situation. It's also something we're still working on! But it's been incredibly empowering and has changed our lives. The more we choose to do this at work and at home, the better decisions we make and the better results we get, and the more impact we have.

However, there have been some massive challenges to our mindset along our journey. In fact, we first heard about this concept about a week before a disaster that severely challenged our new resolve to live from cause: we had a phenomenally terrible "appointment disaster" when the hard drive in our booking computer crashed and our backup also failed. We lost all 250 or so appointments for the upcoming month, both those booked with our staff and the osteopath who was running his business from our rooms.

Elicia was first to discover what had happened, and she was completely gutted. There's that moment of shock, then fear, and then that feeling of horror that throbs in the pit of your stomach. Elicia's reaction was to get angry: angry at our IT guy, angry at James, angry at herself for allowing it to happen, and very, very angry and frustrated at the situation. Our biggest nightmare was that all our clients would see this as evidence that we didn't know what we were doing, and they would leave. Looking back now, this seems so immature, but it was a real feeling that was unearthed by the challenge of the situation.

So anyway, Elicia had a meltdown. Yep. Being responsible for your life does not mean you don't feel, and remember we were pretty new at the whole "from cause" thing at the time. Then Elicia reached out to her mentor and asked, *"What the heck do we do?"* Her mentor said, "What would Richard Branson do? Do you think it's possible he has overcome challenges in his business greater than this, on his journey to running 200 companies?" Then she told Elicia to work out the solution and document everything we did.

So, the next day, Elicia went to work with a plan. She asked the staff, what do you think Richard Branson would do? And they laughed at her. Ocean Grove is a small, tourist-driven coastal town, and our clinic was not exactly Virgin Airlines.

So Elicia took the lead.

"This is what we're going to do. Everyone who needs to can have a meltdown here and now. Rant, get upset, cry. Whatever you need to do to feel the frustration.

"Then, once that is over, this is the action we are taking."

To begin to get everything back on track we paused on new bookings coming in and we manually pieced our diary back together over about two weeks. One of our staff had what seemed like a photographic memory, and so as a team we were able to remember about 30% of our appointments. Then we called everyone, SMSed, emailed, and even put an ad in the local paper explaining what had happened.

Importantly, we also managed the narrative of what had happened. We had a single story that was shared with our clients and our database. That story was: we have lost all our appointments as our hard drive has crashed and our backups have failed. We need to know when your next booking is, if you can remember.

Our biggest challenge would be from accidental double bookings from new people who had booked in but who we didn't have paper-copy details for yet so we couldn't contact them. So we created a "mixed-up appointment" gift pack that included a letter of explanation, a 20% off voucher for their next appointment with us, some products, and a bag of "Mix-up M&Ms". So, when we had a double booking, we had a way of owning it, apologising, and fixing up the mistake.

45

"It always seems impossible until it's done."

Nelson Mandela

The whole team came on board with this plan, and we implemented it like we were possessed. It was stressful and it took more time and energy than normal. But two massive learnings came out of this:

- Of the 250 or so appointments in the next few weeks, only four were double-booked in the end, all of them were new clients, and all of them rescheduled. What seemed at first like an insurmountable disaster turned out to have a workable solution.

- The other amazing learning was that instead of our bookings going down and people leaving like we had feared, the opposite happened. We noticed a massive *increase* in bookings over the next four months. We think this was because we had more contact with everyone in this time, and people paid extra attention to us because we were asking for help. It proved the saying true in this case: "any publicity is good publicity".

Towards the end of the first month post-disaster, Elicia overheard a conversation at the end of a massage. The client was commenting that it must have been hard to get through, and our therapist replied, "Yes, it has been a challenge but we have managed it really well as a team."

At that moment Elicia was filled with pride at how this had been handled, and gratitude for the amazing mindset of all the therapists who had helped pull it off.

Challenges produce strength

You can see from the examples in this chapter that challenges can produce strength if you live from cause and handle them well, rather than being a victim and simply walking away because it's all too hard.

Our experience of owning the appointment disaster and managing it allowed us to grow our business quicker than without it. Jason attracted more clients more quickly because of the skills he learnt in response to competition. Grace also grew her business faster than anticipated because an injury forced her to hire sooner than she would otherwise have been comfortable with.

What is this mystery?

How can it be that situations that feel so incredibly disastrous at the time can have such a positive outcome?

The answer is that it depends entirely on the mindset we take to the challenge.

It's easy for us to get caught up in the moments of challenge and we don't always see the gold, but when we come from cause, we take action and find a way to make it work. And the action we take builds our experience and our character, allowing us to tackle even bigger challenges next time they arise.

Coming from cause is not easy. And the actions you choose to take as you respond to disasters are not easy. But the more you choose to accept responsibility for the situations around you and your business, the more successful you will become.

It all starts with choice.

What will you choose?

CHAPTER 4

SETTING POWERFUL GOALS

Setting a goal for what you want to achieve is a basic business exercise, yet so many people struggle to write goals down clearly, or don't set them at all. In fact, some people avoid even setting a goal in case they never reach it! And often even the people who do set a goal don't do it in a way that inspires them to keep working towards it.

HOW TO SET POWERFUL GOALS

A clear goal is simply a compass point to guide you to what you're after. It guides you as you make decisions and assess opportunities. You know what actions are right because they line up with your vision for your future.

What we'll show you here is the most powerful way you can set a goal so that you have an immediate, super-strong connection with it that will carry you through your action steps until you have reached what you want to achieve. If you've ever written down your goals at all you're already ahead of the game, but without these other steps in place you'll still find it difficult to fulfil your dreams. The powerful part comes from the way you set yourself up to do it so that you get to where you want every time.

Being specific

We all know what it's like to make New Year's resolutions…we say things like, "This year I'm going to lose some weight, or make more money, or save for a holiday, or I'm going to take more days off…" The problem with these goals is they are too vague and wishy-washy. Your brain doesn't know what "more" or "less" actually means. Are you aiming to lose 2 kilograms or 10? Do you want to improve your income by 10% or 40%?

So the first thing we need to do to make our goals powerful is to make them specific.

How much money do you want to be making in the next 12 months? Is that turnover in your business (all the money coming in) or is it the amount of money you want to pay yourself each week after expenses?

If you have health goals and you want to lose weight – how much exactly do you want to lose? If you want to get fitter – what does that look like to you? Do you want to be able to run 5 kilometres, or do you want to be able to survive a PT session without passing out?

Setting a deadline

Once we are being specific about a goal, then we need to add in some timing around it. A deadline. And in order for our brain to accept it in the most powerful way, we state this deadline positively and like it has already happened.

Let us give you some examples:

- *On or before 30th of June this year I have lost 5 kilograms.*

- *On or before 1st January I have started paying myself $1000 per week into my bank account.*

- *On 16th May this year I am running the Great Ocean Road Half Marathon with ease.*

Making it real

Once we have established a specific goal that's measurable and has a timeframe around it, then we need to know what it's going to be like when we get there. This will help our subconscious mind relate to it more deeply. To do this, add in some visual, kinaesthetic, auditory, olfactory and gustatory (VKAOG) parameters as well. This basically means deciding what achieving the goal looks like, feels like, sounds like, smells like and tastes like.

Adding these experiential details makes the goal much more achievable because we have already experienced it in our imagination, so our brain knows exactly what to look for:

On or before 20th June next year I have lost 5 kilos. I am sitting in my clinic and I notice how loose my new jeans feel as I sip my protein shake. I can see my diary and we're fully booked. I sit there and I hear the clicking of the keyboard as I type my notes, and I tell myself it's because of the work I have done at home preparing meals and exercising twice a week in the gym that I am here, so I feel really proud of myself for being consistent.

Do you think the writer of this knows what she's looking for? It's pretty clear, hey?

✪ ✪ ✪

If you fail to set a clear, powerful goal in business or in life it takes longer to get traction as your strategy zigzags, or even worse you wander aimlessly.

Lack of clarity can also lead to feelings of overwhelm and burnout because you keep working and working and doing more and more all the time, and without clear guidelines there's no way to know if you're winning, so it can feel like you're spinning on an endless wheel. The natural desire to help your clients can become a de facto goal, and without other guidelines this can mean you set poor boundaries and sacrifice other parts of your life.

THE PLEDGE

Setting a powerful goal is the first step on the path to reaching success. You've now defined what success actually is for you. Well done!

Now it's time to motivate yourself towards your goal. In a few chapters' time we've got so much practical, tactical advice to give you about what the steps will be as you move there. It's vital that you know what steps to take.

But even more vital than that is *actually taking them*. Taking any good step at all is better than sitting still and not moving towards your compass point.

A personal pledge is a way to identify your own deep motivators and use them to stay motivated to move towards the goal you've set. A deep motivator is basically a big "reason why" you must do what you need to do. Sometimes we're not aware of it in everyday life, but most big decisions we make are driven by internal motivators of some kind, to do with values we hold about who we should be and what we feel is right for us, or how we want our life to be.

Writing your pledge is a way of becoming more aware of these deep motivators and consciously using them to remind you of why you must take action towards your goals. It's like creating your own goal posts, so that you know where to aim and you will know when a goal is achieved.

What pushes your buttons?

You know what pushes your buttons, right? You know what you really care about, deep down. You know what your most powerful motivators are.

Is it your family? Is it paying off the mortgage? Is it buying a new car, or taking a holiday? Maybe setting a solid example as a role model for your children?

Whatever it is, allow it to be meaningful. It's a natural habit when you start thinking about these ideas to make yourself feel better by downplaying how terrible it would feel to lose the house, or reduce how important it is that you give your kids your best time and energy.

For this exercise, instead of comforting yourself... *do the opposite*. Take the mantle of responsibility seriously. Or the fear. Or the hope of a better future.

Whatever drives you the most, allow yourself to really feel it.

When you let it go deep, and you really feel it, these motivators will become even more powerful as drivers of your behaviour.

To do this you may need a few minutes of silence as you dig deep. Then write a pledge that includes some key parts of your goals, along with the reasons why you *must* get these things done. (We've provided an example in the following exercise.)

"Everything is created twice.
First in the mind, then in reality."

Robin Sharma

After you've written your pledge, sign it. Take it seriously. Make a pact with yourself that this is what you're going to do. Your pledge becomes a serious commitment to you that you'll reach your business goal for the year.

We have created pledges each year for the last three years. They get stuck up inside our wardrobe so we'll see them every day, and each year we have used the pledges to help us reach our goals. We want to share here the specific format we use, and invite you to create yours. Make it your own: you will have different motivators and different levels of goals, so make it meaningful to you.

 EXERCISE: MAKE YOUR PLEDGE

Use this example to create your own pledge that is meaningful to you. Make sure you write it on paper or print it out. Stick it on your mirror or inside your wardrobe door, somewhere that you'll see it regularly so you can remind yourself that this is a promise, and you *must take action!*

My Pledge

I, *[NAME]*, pledge to do everything in my power to see *[X]* number of clients and make *[$X]* income on or before *[DATE]*. To empower *[X]* number of clients to grow their businesses and live with passion, growth and contribution. To sponsor 100 children through *[SPECIFIC CHARITY YOU WANT TO SUPPORT]* before the year 2021.

I will be my best, break through fears, take all necessary action and complete every single activity required over the next 12 months. I must succeed as I have my partner, my children and my dad

55

[WRITE DOWN AT LEAST THREE PEOPLE WHO MEAN THE WORLD TO YOU] counting on me, and I must be the best I can be to show people that anything is possible, and life is amazing. This is my purpose, it is my destiny. This is my time and I am ready!

[YOUR NAME]

Date:

Signed:

_____

You can use this same process to create powerful goals and commitments for different areas of your life, such as business, relationships, health, spirituality and finances.

Clarify exactly what you want to see in these areas over the next 12 months, and who you get to be when the goals are met. Once you know your outcome, you can break it down to quarterly, monthly and weekly steps.

Then the action starts.

CHAPTER 5

LOOKING AFTER YOURSELF

Once you've got a handle on your own motivation and have oriented yourself towards action (or maybe you are someone who is already good at that), you might find it feels really good to put your head down and work hard. It actually can feel really great to work super hard for a few days or even weeks, pulling late nights and early mornings to get through the list of tasks you're now so motivated to work on. The sense of achievement can be addictive.

But this crazy, adrenaline-fuelled pace is not sustainable long term, and doesn't lead to a holistically fulfilling life. To fulfil the needs you have across your entire life and enhance your daily experience of existing in the world, you need to give time and energy to looking after yourself.

And the best thing is... when you create a balanced life where you are looking after yourself, this in itself becomes another way that you can influence your clients and your community towards better health.

When you set the standard for yourself, you become a role model for those around you.

In this way, when you live an inspired life, you begin to step into the role of Health Leader.

CARING FOR THE CAREGIVER

As a massage therapist, you have the unique opportunity – and gift – that you get to physically touch people more in a standard 60-minute treatment than any other health professional. You can connect with a bunch of different people every day in this powerful way. This is an incredible joy, and every day you can hear stories of how clients' lives have been changed through massage treatments.

But… what can happen is that eventually treating people in this way takes a toll. You can become tired and stressed, and if you're not looking after yourself you may feel drained by the energy and care you give to others.

This is why taking care of "you" is so important.

It's like filling your own cup so you can overflow into others. It's like putting on your oxygen mask in a plane before helping those around you.

This is what prevents burnout.

Imagine that "self-care" is like a bank account. If you put more money in than you need, you start to save and see yourself grow. If you take out more than you put in, you get a deficit.

In our experience, people fear "burnout" far more than they actually experience it. But even the fear of it can stop you from performing at your best. So why wait until it happens? You can put things in place in your life to prevent it before it happens. There are five areas of self-care we're going to share about here that have been vital throughout Elicia's 17-year career as a therapist, and have enabled her to stay injury-free and still be passionate about what she does.

Even when practising these, it doesn't mean you'll never been tired or get sore hands or go too long before taking a holiday. But with these practices in place you will prevent some of the negative feelings that can arise when you experience the first niggles of burnout, and see this as something to work through rather than feeling like you need to tap out.

IT'S ALL ABOUT YOU

As a therapist you are an athlete.

Your ability to keep working and treating long term with the same or better outcomes relies solely on how well you take care of yourself. Just like an elite athlete has to do certain things to maintain a level of fitness to compete, so do you.

The average career of a therapist is three years. But we'd love it to be much longer! If you are going to do this for 5, 10 or even 20 years or more, then you need to have a self-care routine every day to invest in you.

You only get one body. And as a therapist you're good at talking to your clients about their self-care – now you need to listen to your own message. By simply recognising the importance of looking after yourself, you're on the path to finding the exact habits and routines that will sustain you through a long and healthy career.

MOVE IT

If we can continue with the athlete theme, the next step is to ensure that you are moving your body to keep physically fit in a way that will encourage longevity in the industry. For example, if you are

59

treating 20 to 30 clients a week for a large chunk of the year, you're going to be putting excess load on your upper body. So weight lifting or boxing might not be the best path to choose to keep fit.

When you do a workout or exercise regime, leave extra time for stretching out your upper body, and strengthen your shoulder external rotators with a theraband. Maybe see a personal trainer or exercise physiologist and ask them to create a strengthening program that you can work on to open up your body.

Also as you increase your activity, remember the importance of great rest and sleep. Your body does a lot of cellular repair at night. If you can, plan out an early night or sleep-in from time to time; this is such a beautiful form of self-care.

As well as being useful for your physical health, your fitness journey can become brilliant content to post on social media. It's inspirational living. You are a Health Leader, so when you're making great choices you can share that. Your clients and your community need to hear about it.

KEEP CALM AND CARRY ON

Earlier we looked at how to stay motivated and in control of your mindset. This is a very active energy and extremely beneficial for growing your business and yourself.

The thing is, your mind also needs times of self-care so that you can stay calm and happy. Scheduling time in your calendar to recharge your mental batteries is just as important as looking after your body. The two are intimately connected.

As a business owner you may sometimes place expectations on yourself to stay motivated and complete lots of tasks every day and week to move you forward more quickly on your journey. We know that we do! It can feel great, and it moves you forward fast. But if you live in this energy too much and don't allow yourself times of calm, it can also lead to more stress and anxiety in your daily life. This in turn affects your body as well as your mind.

So how do you stay highly motivated and proactive in your mindset, and still create enough space for your mental health? The secret is to practise moments of calm regularly, and create this as a thought habit within your mind.

One way to purposefully build calm and clarity into your life is through mindfulness meditation. A daily mindfulness meditation is designed to increase self-awareness so that moments of mindful awareness are experienced throughout the day. This improves connection with people around you and the world we live in.

We use a short daily mindfulness practice ourselves, and James especially has experienced massive benefits from it. With a morning meditation of only 10 minutes it has increased the number of "mindful moments" that he experiences each day and given him regular feelings of more calm in his thoughts and a stronger emotional connection with other people. It also has practical benefits: he has better focus at work, his memory is improving, and he doesn't get as angry at our dog when she digs up his garden.

You may also find that any break you have from the hustle and bustle of work helps you to feel calmer and happier. Be aware of your own mental state and note when you feel really good. Was it after a beach walk? Or chatting with friends? Taking a holiday? The secret is to catch yourself in moments of calm and happiness, and to focus on those feelings when you have them. Experience each special moment with full presence, as powerfully as you can, and it will fill you up even more.

Then make time to do it again as often as you need.

USEFUL TOOL: INSIGHT TIMER

If you would like to experiment with mindfulness or other forms of meditation, download the free "Insight Timer" app on your phone. This app has a library of thousands of guided meditations you can listen to, including "mindfulness" and many other forms. It also has a simple timer function that plays soft background sounds or music for a length of time you choose if you want to try it without voices. Try a meditation for at least 10 minutes each morning for a week and notice how you feel.

YOU ARE WHAT YOU EAT

Food is fuel for the body. The better you eat, the better it's going to run.

We're not going to talk about rabbit food diets or crazy eating plans here – there's plenty of other places you can learn more about that, from people more qualified than us in this area. Instead, our invitation for you is to begin to notice how the food you eat affects your energy levels when you're treating. For example, do you feel like a sleep after lunch? Do you struggle to recover after a big day? This can be due to the fuel you're putting in.

What we have noticed with ourselves and by observing our teams that we have led in our businesses is that some people had more energy and consistency on a regular basis. These were the people who planned out their meals, brought healthy leftovers for lunch, and fruit, nuts, and protein shakes for snacks. The ones who ducked to the shop for a pie and lollies did not cope as well. There are so many different ways to eat and diets to follow: wholefoods, high protein, intermittent fasting, the blood group diet, Lite n' Easy, vegan, gluten free, sugar free, Jenny Craig, counting calories… you name it, there is probably a "diet and eating plan" for it.

If one of these works for you, and fills you with energy for your day, then great! Stick with it and reap the benefits. If you have trouble following a really structured plan then keep it simple and notice what is happening with the energy levels in your body as you experiment with different foods. The best thing to do is to listen to the feelings within your own body and eat right for you, your body and your energy needs. The last thing you need is more stress, so keep it simple. It's well established by research that fresher, less processed foods with more fruit and vegetables give you more energy. And just like you might speak to a personal trainer to help with an exercise plan, you can speak with a nutritionist, naturopath, GP or someone else you trust to get the right food advice for you and your body.

Hydration is another really important factor in your daily energy and overall health. But we probably don't need to tell you that – you would understand the importance of hydration on your clients' muscles and how super important it is to drink at least two litres a day. Water hydrates your digestive tract, gives moisture to your eyes and nasal passages, helps to plump out your red blood cells – which allows oxygen to flow through the body better – and also it makes it easier for the blood to flow through your muscles and keep them working well as you treat.

Also, just because you're a Health Leader doesn't mean you need to eat a perfect diet or look a certain way. Food is for enjoyment as well as nourishment. A Mars Bar can be okay too!

KEEP IT FAST AND EFFECTIVE

People sometimes say to us that they don't have enough time for self-care or can't afford to do it because it's too expensive. But simple, fast and cheap self-care is still effective if you do it right.

So we've created a list here with self-care ideas to get you started. This list is for people who do not have lots of time for self-care (which, let's be honest, is pretty much everyone). So we've made them really quick ideas.

We've also put in lots of ideas that are less than $30, or totally free. So if finances are a stretch for you right now (which is often the case as you're building your business), you can still practise many of these fabulous activities to feed your own soul.

Now before you start, this is important: part of the trick here is to be mindful of your purpose as you use these techniques – tell yourself that this is part of your self-care routine and that what you're doing is refilling your tanks. It hardly matters what activity you're actually doing. As long as you make it meaningful to you, it will work.

 EXERCISE: 50 SIMPLE THINGS YOU CAN DO TO FEEL GOOD

Here's 50 simple things you can do which will make you feel good and don't take much time at all:

1. Treat yourself by going out for afternoon tea.
2. Watch an inspirational YouTube video.
3. Take a mindful walk around the block, breathing deeply.
4. Get a manicure.
5. Plant a flower in your garden or planter.

6. Get a pedicure.

7. Pat your dog.

8. See a beauty therapist.

9. Look up inspirational images on Pinterest and daydream about remodelling your kitchen.

10. Write a pen-and-paper letter to someone you care about but don't see often.

11. YouTube your favourite song from when you were 16, play it loud, and dance like a crazy teenager.

12. Go for a run.

13. Get dressed up for a great reason.

14. Get someone else to clean, iron or cook for you.

15. Draw a really good picture. (Gifting it to your mum is optional!)

16. Take an afternoon nap.

17. Attend a health expo or market.

18. Make a cup of tea and sit and enjoy it until it's all gone, without your phone.

19. Sleep in… zzzzz.

20. Go to a local farmers' market and look a producer in the eye while you buy their vegetables.

21. Walk barefoot through the park.

22. Take a bath.

23. Sit in the sun (and remember to slip, slop, slap).

24. Go out for coffee.

25. Play sport (basketball, tennis, hockey, volleyball).

26. Go for a swim in the ocean.

27. Buy a new pair of shoes.

28. Meet a friend for coffee and gossip.

29. Attend a Zumba class.

30. Cook a special meal that your mum used to make when you were a kid.

31. Join in some laughter therapy.

32. Sew something.

33. Read some excellent poetry. Aloud!

34. Hang out with your family.

35. Buy something silly on eBay.

36. Get dressed up for no reason at all.

37. Go 10-pin bowling.

38. Go to the gym.

39. Get up early and watch the sunrise.

40. Listen to an audiobook or podcast.

41. Watch your favourite DVD.

42. Photograph something cool.

43. Give someone you care about a big hug.

44. Meet a friend for drinks.

45. Go roller-skating or ice-skating.

46. Zone out on Facebook.

47. Read a book.

48. Listen to some awesome music.

49. Get a haircut.

50. Call someone you love, just to chat.

In the end, your health and longevity in the industry is going to be largely dependent on how well you can care for yourself, in whatever way that is.

Care for yourself in ways that resonate with you.

You deserve it for yourself.

And you owe it to your clients and your community.

PART II

AMAZING MARKETING

CHAPTER 6

THE FUNDAMENTALS

Marketing is absolutely vital for growing your massage business. It gives your clients a consistently amazing experience even before they step through your door. We love that there are so many tools available now to get the word out about your business. The sophistication of what has developed has made marketing so much easier and more powerful than when we first started over 16 years ago. For example, Facebook is more than just social media: it's an extraordinary tool to get your message out to more people, unparalleled in its effectiveness and affordability.

However, all of these great opportunities are platforms that don't do any magic on their own. Similar to a loudhailer, they help your message reach more people, but a loudhailer doesn't change what the message itself is. Imagine giving a loudhailer to a monkey... all it would do is allow the monkey to annoy more people.

When you use any sort of social media or other marketing tool you are using a loudhailer, so having a clear and compelling message is most important. Before going loud and wide, ensure it is the right message so that you are connecting authentically with more people. Instead of being a monkey, you will have a powerful, appealing message that will be heard by a larger audience.

YOUR MARKETING FUNNEL

Before we get into the tactics of exactly what to do with your social media, website, and print advertising (and all the rest of it), we want to give this conversation some context and introduce some basic terminology by showing you a "marketing funnel".

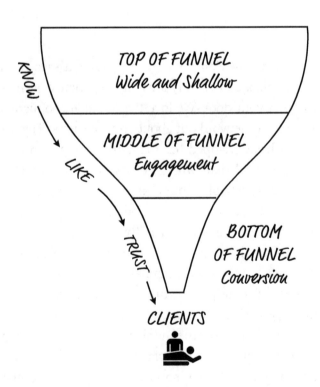

If you've done any kind of marketing study before you may have seen this; it's a fantastic tool that shows how the different parts of your marketing fit together into a system, and it reveals very clearly why some people have more success than others when doing similar marketing activities: you need to have tactics in place at each part of the funnel system for it to work most effectively.

Let me explain how it works.

Wide and shallow

At the top, we have what we call your "wide and shallow" marketing activities. These include social media posts, online adverts, getting found on Google, and other bits and pieces where people may see something of yours. It's a quick and simple interaction.

These top-of-funnel activities may go out to thousands of people, but each activity has only a very small impact. That's why we call it wide and shallow.

Building engagement

Top-of-funnel activity builds knowledge of who you are, so that people become more familiar with you and your core messages. However, the real purpose of this activity is to get people to click through to something more substantial. This is the middle of your funnel, and this is where your audience can engage with you on something that's a little meatier. They might read an article, watch a slightly longer video, or explore your services. The middle of the funnel most often involves a visit to your website, although you could have a Facebook page or an event or something similar that fills this position in the funnel. Whatever it looks like, your tribe are learning to like you more, to feel as if they have more than just knowledge, and are starting to align themselves with who you are and the mission you have for your business.

Becoming a client

The final step in the funnel is where these people "convert" to become paying clients and book in for a treatment. At this point they trust you enough to want to experience what you do, by booking online, calling you by phone or connecting in another way.

The basic idea is that lots of people see the things that happen at the top of the funnel – the social media, the adverts – but only some of those people will actually act on it to click through. For example, out of every thousand people who see a Facebook ad, fifty might click through. Then they take a look around your website, see what you do, maybe read an article you wrote or watch a video or two so they can get a feel for the kind of person you are and the business you run. Then they naturally feel it if they are a fit and will take the final step to book in. Of every fifty that visit your website, maybe five will be ready at that moment to take the step to book in.

This is why it's called a "funnel", because it's larger at the top and the number of people at each stage gets smaller as it goes down.

Now, sometimes a person's journey through this funnel might be very simple – like when an individual searches Google, clicks to your website and books online immediately. When this happens it's great, as it is a sign to you that you have each step in that funnel pathway working well. But to build a stronger and more consistent business, you want to work on filling all parts of the funnel more fully. There should be lots of people who are at the top, seeing wide and shallow material from you so that they know who you are.

From there, you need to develop a strong middle of the funnel, so that plenty of people can connect more fully and learn to love what it is you stand for. When this group is large enough there are always people who will be ready to experience your services and trust you at that level, and we want to ensure it's as easy as possible for them to take that step when it's time.

This is what we call "growing your tribe", because when you have a group of people who all align themselves behind you and your business, it creates loyalty and momentum in your business. There is consistency and security in having a tribe around you, plus it is affirmation that what you are doing is helping and inspiring more people as you become a Health Leader for them.

So now you can see how important all the steps in the funnel are, and you can also identify why some people seem to find marketing so difficult. Even if you're a superhero at social media or have an amazing reputation locally, if the middle or bottom of your marketing funnel is sloppy you won't get the same level of actual bookings that you could otherwise.

GROWING YOUR TRIBE

Even the most amazing product in the world won't sell if no-one knows what it is or they don't trust the promise of the person selling it. That's why it's important to have a group of followers and fans who know who you are, trust what you say, and love what you do – so that you can feed the top of your funnel effectively.

Having a tribe around you is like greasing the wheel of your marketing. Everything flows more easily when you already have momentum with your audience. And when it comes to being a Health Leader, part of the purpose of that role is influencing your community – leading your tribe into better health through inspiration and education.

And to do that you need followers.

Social media and your tribe

In today's world, social media is a massive tool for connecting with your audience. It can be used to share practical information, to enable bookings or sales, and to share personal inspiration. It's also an incredibly targeted way to learn about your niche and what content they like.

So what happens if you feel nervous using social media? Remember, this is why we started with mindset. There are other things you can use to attract clients of course, but they are mostly slower, less effective, and more expensive. (And not as much fun!) Instead, even if you haven't done much on social media before, this may be your opportunity to broaden your experience now that you have a practical purpose for it.

Look at it this way: when someone is with you for a treatment they'll see your face and hear your voice. In fact, it's a huge part of the way you make a strong connection with them and help them feel comfortable with you. You'll also use that connection to give them health advice and help them on their way. All you're doing by being active and open on social media is bringing that moment forward in time, and using the same skills you have naturally in person in order to connect with people before they even come in.

When you share regularly on social media you reveal a much more personal side to your business that gives people a more authentic insight into who you are and why you do what you do. Over time, you'll connect with more and more people in your community and build up a tribe of people who follow you and align with your beliefs and values.

Some of your tribe will form very strong bonds with you and become true friends as you get to know them more. Your relationships with others will be a lot lighter, and that's natural within the tribe too. The most important thing is that you are regularly and consistently being seen so you can become known, liked and trusted.

DEVELOPING CONSISTENT BRANDING

Imagine if every time you met one of your friends she had a different face. It would be difficult to recognise her, right? And if she wasn't a close friend, but just an acquaintance, then it would be even more difficult to remember who she was.

If your business has inconsistent branding then it creates the same problem. Your audience can't recognise who you are as easily, especially in an environment where they are most likely not focusing particularly hard on you and your business. In extreme cases we see businesses that use different logos in different places; for example, with different graphics, fonts, colours or words. Recently James spoke to a man who had a different "version" of his logo on his business card compared to his website, and his shirt had an entirely different logo again. His business has different faces, and it's confusing.

Consistency means you look the same in every place where someone will see you. And this goes beyond just your logo. You should also be consistent with the words you use, your colour palette, the style of photography, your fonts, and everything else that presents your business to potential clients. This is true "branding", where every way that a client can be in touch with your business presents a consistent experience for them that introduces and supports your core messages and services. Even your clinic space should carry through the same look and feel so that it enhances your brand even more.

How do you know what style to use for your visual design? The look and feel of your branding should support your core message and connect with your tribe. Each part of the process hooks together to produce a crazily powerful connection.

CHAMPION SNAPSHOT: HAZEL CHEE

Hazel bought a small day spa when she started working with us, and it used the name and brand that matched another location the previous owner was still running. So, it was very important for Hazel to create a new look so she could separate her business and show her unique style.

Hazel used a graphic designer who created a fabulous new logo, and Hazel rolled it out across her business, replacing everything from business cards and brochures through to giant wall art. The transformation was spectacular, and the result is a new level of professionalism that is often commented on by earlier clients and is a beautiful foundation for all the marketing done to attract new people.

IDENTIFYING YOUR TARGET AUDIENCE

Now let's return to this idea of your core message. Remember how important we said this is? None of your marketing will work if your message doesn't connect with your tribe. And a message to everyone is a message to no-one. So how do you make sure your message is on point?

The secret is to be very specific about who your target audience is and what you do for them. And this starts with knowing yourself intimately and identifying the big "why" behind what you do.

Why are you a massage therapist? What are t[training or unique skills that you bring to the tabl to go as deep as you need to with this, because yc to ensure that your business aligns with your deep desires. When you use your highest values to guide your business creation it means you experience much higher levels of fulfilment as you achieve your purpose.

An invaluable tactic here is to create an "avatar" of your ideal client. This means you create a profile of a single individual person that is right at the centre of your target audience. Give them a name, age, family status, and anything else that is relevant. Then write a few sentences about what problem they have that you help to solve. Be as specific as you can; this is a single person you are creating, not a range.

The reason we suggest you do this is twofold. Firstly, it helps incredibly with clarity. Creating a single avatar forces you to think about what the biggest problem you solve is, and what you need to leave out. Secondly, it helps you be more direct and personal so that you can connect more powerfully. You'll find that having a single person in mind when you're creating your marketing makes it easier to speak in the right tone, to choose your images, and even to define your services.

⬭ TIP: AVATAR IDENTIFIER

To help create your ideal client avatar with even more clarity, think about your favourite three to five real clients. What problems did they present with? How did you help them? What do they have in common? The answers become the foundation for your client avatar and help you attract more of those type of people.

Now this doesn't mean you can't serve other people – of course you still can, and will. Your "target" doesn't need to be your entire client base. Other people will book in and you'll do a great job treating them. The purpose of having a target is so you can craft your marketing and your growth more specifically and powerfully.

DIRECT RESPONSE AND CONTENT MARKETING

There's basically two different philosophies when it comes to running your marketing and advertising, and they exist at opposite ends of the same spectrum:

- The first is what we call "direct response" marketing. This means you are using your marketing to try to get your audience to do something right away when they see it. For example, if you pay for an advert in the local newspaper you might want people to come in and book immediately. You can judge the success of the advert based on how many direct responses it creates.

- At the opposite end of the marketing spectrum we have "content marketing". This is where you create useful content that educates or entertains people so that they get to know you more and become familiar with your message. When your tribe know you well by being more involved with what you are publishing, you become a more obvious choice for them when it comes time to select a therapist.

In a way, marketing is like catching fish. To catch fish in a pond, first you throw out a bunch of food to get the fish milling around. Then you scoop the net to catch the fish.

In this analogy, content marketing is like throwing out the food. You feed your audience with your Facebook and Instagram posts, blog articles, videos, emails, and anything else you can create that will help solve their problems and build your reputation. As you climb the Health Leader Ladder you can even include meatier content like a podcast or book.

Most of your content marketing sits in the middle step of your funnel. People can read or watch it to learn more about you and what you stand for. This is sometimes called "helpful marketing" because you want to be as helpful as you can to your tribe so they will like and trust you.

Then your direct response marketing is like scooping the net. This is where you have an obvious call to action like "click here to book" or "call now", and it often happens through some of your social media posts and paid advertising.

The thing we love about this fishing analogy is that it shows how these activities work together. You need to scoop in order to get clients. And the scooping is far more effective once plenty of fish have been attracted.

In essence, we always recommend that you do both forms of marketing to create a long-term sustainable business. But if you're at the start of your journey you're going to do more direct response to get your early clients quickly and easily. Then, as you move up the ladder you'll need to create more high-value content in order to spread your audience wider and build more trust.

WHAT TO SPEND ON MARKETING

How much should you spend on marketing? This is a question we get regularly, and the answer is: something!

So many people fall into the trap of thinking that they only want to do free marketing activities. This may be because they don't have much cashflow when they are starting out, or due to a misguided thought that paying for marketing or advertising to get clients somehow devalues their actual service. We hear people say things like, "If I'm a good enough therapist then people will hear about me and book in". But the problem with this is that they're ignoring exactly "how" those people are going to hear about their services.

You can't rely on word-of-mouth referrals until you have a tribe of clients who can go out and share about you – no good at all if you're just starting and don't have many clients yet! And even when you do have a client base, referrals are hard to influence. If you look at your calendar for next week and realise you need some more clients … you can't do much to make referrals happen. So instead of passively waiting for other people to do your marketing for you, take control of your business by proactively learning, doing and growing. Ultimately, relying on free marketing limits your growth and is the most time-consuming and difficult way to gain new clients.

But how much should you spend?

Cost per client acquisition

We'll be looking at strategies later in this book that are great value for money (and yes, some are free). However, we want to introduce you to a different way of looking at your marketing budget.

Rather than looking at marketing as a general business expense ("I've got $50 to spend on marketing this week"), we want you to shift to thinking of it as a "per-new-client" expense ("It cost me $20 to get this client in the door"). This is what we call the "client acquisition cost" – it's a simple measure of how much we spent on advertising or marketing to "acquire" that client the first time. For example, if you spend $50 advertising on Google for a week and during that week you get five bookings from this advertising, that's a $10 acquisition cost for each client. Or if you run a local newspaper advert for $100 and you get two phone calls out of it, that is a $50 acquisition cost.

Average lifetime value

Now $50 might seem very high to get someone in for a single treatment... and it is, if they only come in once. But clients usually come several times. When Elicia was training she was taught that most people will need one to three treatments to resolve their condition – and many will go on to maintenance plans after that. To work out more clearly what acquisition cost is acceptable for your business, you need to look at the lifetime value of your average client. This goes beyond their very first treatment and looks at how many sessions people usually receive from you and what else they might buy from you over that time.

If you look through your past clients and can see that an average treatment plan goes for three sessions and then about half of those clients go on to receive monthly maintenance treatments then you can predict that any new client might see you on average nine times in their first year. If you charge $85 per treatment then that's an average lifetime value of $765 (nine treatments multiplied by $85). So spending $50 to acquire a client is totally reasonable.

As a rule of thumb, you can spend up to 10% of the lifetime value on acquiring a client, although the less you spend the better of course. So with the example lifetime value of $765 it would be okay to spend $76.50 on client acquisition.

This figure is actually quite high, and even a poorly performing marketing campaign should be able to achieve better than this. We see therapists commonly being happy with acquiring new clients for from $0 using free methods to $35 for paid adverts, and anywhere across that range is a great result. Obviously the lower the number the better, as long as you are getting the results you want and it's not taking too much time and energy.

"No matter what you do,
your job is to tell your story."

Gary Vaynerchuk

Testing, measuring and improving your results

You can increase your average lifetime value from each client by improving your rebooking skills and having products or other services that you provide. This allows you to spend even more attracting new people or to take home more profit. Both great outcomes! This may sound like a lot of numbers and statistics but it's really quite simple to measure, and some booking software will automatically show you these figures, which makes it super easy.

Once you know your ideal acquisition cost you can look at how many clients you want to attract each week and budget accordingly. If you want four new clients each week and you know your average acquisition cost is $20, you should budget $80 in total.

Remember to ask each new client where they heard of you so that you can track each advertising campaign or marketing channel separately. This is vital so you know how much it is costing you for clients from each of your marketing efforts. Then you can compare, test, measure and adjust as needed. Often you'll be aiming for an acquisition cost far below the 10%, but use that as an upper limit.

BECOMING A LOCAL PERSONALITY

Being a Health Leader means more than just performing treatments on your clients. And it's not just about your personal business goals. To lead people you must become known and have an influence on how people live their lives. You need to become a "local personality" by being well known and trusted as a health provider. Once you know your purpose and your "why", you are obligated to live that purpose out and be that positive influence on the people around you.

If you want to make your community healthier, you must become better known and well liked within the tribe you are influencing. When they like you and follow you, they will listen to your advice, see how you live, and make changes to their unhealthy behaviour. This influence can have a massive impact on individuals and change the face of entire communities. And luckily this fits perfectly with your marketing goals too, where having a loyal tribe brings you more clients and is fantastic for business.

One of the first things you need to do in order to have more influence is overcome any nerves or hesitation you have about being seen and known. It's more common than you might think, but here's the thing: being reserved and nervous in this way doesn't serve anyone. Keeping to yourself doesn't help your community learn what they need to do, it doesn't inspire anyone, and it doesn't help your business grow. So, take action within your local community to become better known. This could mean a number of practical activities:

- join clubs or groups and participate or volunteer

- run events at the local neighbourhood centre

- frequent a local café and get to know the manager

- have your own street signage (where appropriate)

- advertise in the local paper or newsletter – these publications often have loyal followings and are well connected within local communities

- provide vouchers to a local school, gym or church – supporting local causes builds your community and is a fabulous way to give back support while building your own reputation.

Whatever it looks like for you, it's about being strong enough to build the muscle of leadership and overcome any nagging social anxiety in the process. You owe it to your clients, your family and yourself to take the action required to make this business successful.

Be courageous. Stand up and stand out. You can do it!

CHAPTER 7

HOW TO BECOME A SOCIAL MEDIA SUPERSTAR

Social media is the most powerful marketing tool available on the planet right now. And Facebook is the most powerful social media. It has billions of users, and in Western countries up to two-thirds of the population actively use it.

HOW TO MAKE THE MOST OF FACEBOOK

So many people we speak to are aware that Facebook is important, but they are either not sure how to approach it themselves or are trying to use it but seeing very few results. Trying to figure it out yourself can be disheartening because Facebook changes regularly and business posts play second fiddle behind friends and family in people's feeds.

The good news is, you can still get results using your free page and paid advertising, and it doesn't have to be hard! Basically, all the different interactions and engagements you can have on Facebook fall into four categories when we look at how they connect with your ideal audience and drive your business growth:

1 research

2 connection and engagement

3 partnerships

4 sales.

We call this the Facebook Cycle, and you'll have the most success on Facebook (and other social media) if you complete each of these phases in order. Let's have a look at each.

1. Research

The very first step in any social media campaign is to understand the people you are connecting with. By being truly connected you gain insights into who they are and how you can help them, plus you will hear their language and see how they talk so that you can communicate even more easily and clearly with them. You'll see how you can put your message into their words so that they take it on board smoothly.

 TIP: MOVE QUICKLY

Remember to move out of the research phase quickly and test your findings by taking action. Otherwise you risk getting stuck in "analysis paralysis" and never seeing the benefits of the research you're doing.

Facebook is the perfect place to learn more about the people you are speaking with. Virtually every adult is on it, and many of them leave their privacy settings open so that information about them and the content they are sharing and publishing is publicly available.

Facebook also makes it incredibly easy to do research. One of the most mind-blowing techniques we show people is how the "smart search" works in Facebook. You know the search bar at the top of the Facebook page? Beyond just searching for your friends or topics, you can perform a "smart search" in this box, meaning you can ask Facebook a question using a specific sentence structure, and it will answer your question (rather than simply searching for the words you enter).

A simple example of this would be if you're working with health-conscious women. You know already that many of your audience like celebrity chef Pete Evans, so into the search box on Facebook you type the exact words "people who like Pete Evans" (it should drop down an autocomplete box as you're typing Pete's name).

As a result of this search, Facebook will give you a list of people who like Pete Evans. Even better, in the sidebar is a box that will let you limit this search only to people in your suburb. Yes, you can actually see a list of people in your suburb who like any given topic. You can only see what they set to be public within their profile, but you'll be amazed at how many people leave their profiles totally open for everyone to see.

What does this do for you? Click through to even just a handful of people in this list and you're seeing the feed of your target audience. You can see exactly what they are sharing, commenting on, lol-ing at, and more. This is research of the best kind because as you notice patterns of how they communicate and what they care about, you can see exactly what to use as content in your own feed. You can see what they like, and use that to form your posting strategy. This is a gold-class method for sourcing content for your page.

The next smart search step is even more powerful. In this step we use Facebook's own algorithm to do some sophisticated quantitative research for us, as we use it to cross-reference all the people that we know are in our audience and discover what other common interests they have.

In the search box this time, type the exact words "Interests liked by people who like Chef Pete Evans". Again, the very last section should give you a dropdown for your interest.

What this smart search does is look at the entire group of people we were just exploring, and it gives you a list of all the interests they have in common. Again, this is an incredible way of seeing what your audience is actively interested in on Facebook and can therefore give you an insight into the topics you should be sharing about.

One thing to note is that it doesn't put them in the exact order of most common to least common interests. Facebook is smarter than that, so it's trying to put them in what it thinks is the order you will most care about. You'll find that the things at the top of the list are topics that you personally "like" through your own Facebook profile, but as you scroll down you'll see other topics that are interests from the rest of the group.

As well as these specific "smart search" tactics, don't underestimate the power of observation when using Facebook in general. Join local community groups and watch what people talk about. You'll find yourself observing the activity going on around you in a whole new way as you filter it with the eyes of creating engaging content.

2. Connection and engagement

Once you have researched and discovered who your audience is and how they behave online, the next step is to connect with them.

This is where the majority of your time and effort will be spent in social media, outside of paying for advertising. Creating a large and highly engaged audience has huge benefits over time as it boosts knowledge of who you are and familiarity with your message. The more people that know you and love what you stand for, the more will respond by taking the next steps to book in for treatment.

Most commonly, engagement through Facebook is centred around the free posting strategy you use on your business page. The posts you put out from here will appear in the feeds of your followers where they can then react to the post, comment on it or share it. As a basic metric to measure you can see that the more reactions, comments and shares you get, the better.

So how do you get more engagement?

We'll look at this in the posting strategy section coming up. But in brief, the way to get more engagement is to create engaging content and truly connect with the people who will become your ideal clients.

This might seem quite zen, but it's the truth: when you focus on what your audience wants, needs, and is passionate about, then you will find yourself posting things that hit the spot for them every time.

Don't overlook one of the other key goals in Facebook engagement, which is to connect with your current and past clients (not just new ones).

Having your clients follow your page and then posting from it regularly is a natural and simple way to stay in their minds and encourage rebooking and referrals. It also gives you a platform to help your clients create more effective change in their lives, as you can motivate and educate them in between treatments.

For both existing and potential clients, your Facebook page is one of the simplest ways to share your message and connect.

3. Partnerships

Leveraging someone else who already has a huge following is the best way to reach your ideal clients on Facebook if they are not yet following your page. This is an explosive strategy that can take your social media into the stratosphere really quickly when it happens the right way.

The actual partnership can look like whatever works for you both as a win–win. It's important to see what you can offer the other partner so that the benefits are seen both ways. If you are already in a business relationship then there may be an obvious way to extend this onto social so that it benefits everyone. For example, if you pay rent that is based on a percentage of your income, which might happen if you rent in a gym or chiropractic studio, then it is in your landlord's best interest to help you get booked out, so regular promotions through their social media accounts will benefit both of you. (And hopefully they'll help out in other ways too.)

In other cases, a similar partnership will be with a business or individual that is not as connected with you. For example, you might chat with a local personal trainer or beauty therapist and offer to cross-promote – you do a few posts about them and they do the same for you.

Another idea is if you can connect with the leader of local sports clubs or other groups, and can offer a group incentive or discount. For example, if you offer a special package for runners in the lead up to a local marathon, you can often find local running groups that operate through Facebook that will be happy to promote you, if you approach them. They get the benefit of being able to offer value to their members that they couldn't get elsewhere, and you get the benefit of an endorsement from a trusted group leader.

Simply sharing posts from other local businesses that align with your target audience is another basic way to build partnerships and connect with the community.

Whatever the case, keep on the lookout for how you can partner with local influencers that match your vision and values, to create win–win benefits for everyone.

4. Sales

The final step we can take with our strategy on Facebook is actually the real reason we use Facebook at all for business. This is where we make sales.

Contrary to what some people will tell you, it's perfectly fine and natural to make sales and advertise your services on Facebook. The thing that some people get wrong, and the reason that social media gets bad press as a sales platform, is that some people don't have the complete ecosystem. Try jumping in to sell online before you have gone through the first two phases of research and engagement and you'll quickly discover that people zone out and don't listen. Your ads cost the earth and no-one responds anyway. Many a business owner has tried social selling too soon and instead found themselves shunned by the people they are trying to sell to.

Think of courting your clients the same way you would court a new partner in life. You are on the lookout for the special someone that will be your life partner and long-term love. You can imagine the very first steps of this romantic relationship might happen by meeting someone at a party or in a group of friends. You talk, get along well, share some common interests. There's a spark.

Now imagine 20 minutes after meeting them for the first time, you ask that person to marry you. "Will you commit to me, to being together forever?" It's not how relationships work. It's too soon to commit.

Instead, if you want to develop a successful relationship, when you meet your potential perfect partner at a party, you chat, you get to know them, and you ask if they'd like to meet for a coffee the next day. You walk home together. You share your stories. You meet the parents. (And maybe the kids.) You progress through the steps of building a relationship and ensuring you are a match for each other before stepping into a deep commitment.

Selling is exactly the same. If you are going to ask them to commit to becoming a client, you need to take it step by step, and not lean in for the pash too fast!

Once you have recognised the place of sales in your holistic Facebook strategy you can look at the specific ways you can sell on Facebook (which are discussed below).

 EXERCISE: AUDIT YOUR FEED

Are you already on Facebook? You can do this simple exercise to get a better understanding of how your feed looks to those who follow you.

Go back over your last 20 posts (either scroll down your page or look under the "Insights" tab), and for each one note down which of the above four categories it falls into. Are you heavily skewed in selling? That could be why your reach is low. Not enough photos of you and your team personally? Engagement and client bookings will suffer.

Ideally, most of your posts should be about connection and engagement, with regular sales posts sprinkled throughout. Take a look at your current feed and then adjust your plan for the future.

IS THERE LIFE OUTSIDE FACEBOOK?

The good news is, these four phases are just as relevant to other social media, so even if you're using Instagram or Snapchat or the next new and exciting social platform, the same basic steps will ensure you are getting the most out of your business social media. This is important, because things change quickly online. Facebook doesn't look like it's going anywhere soon, but even if it did, when you have a powerful message that connects you are guaranteed to find the next way to get to your audience, and you'll be able to pick up where you left off. Okay, so what do I do on Facebook to get clients?

So now you have seen the concept of the Facebook Cycle and know where the different activities you will perform fit into the strategy for business growth. It's time to get into some ticky-tacks and look at what you will actually do on Facebook to roll through that cycle.

Setting up your business page

Posting on Facebook from your business page is the primary way you will connect with your audiences on this platform. Your business page is an important asset for your business on Facebook. It's actually not the place that people will see you the most – more often your followers will see your material as they scroll through their own feed. (So they'll see your posts in between photos of cats, lunches and their nephew Johnnie with yoghurt all over his face.) But your page is the vehicle you use to put those posts out there, and if someone clicks through to learn more about you it's important to give them the best experience possible. So set up your business page for success by making it professional, friendly, and consistent with your core marketing messages.

To make it more useful to followers, use photos and messages that match your brand, and fill in all the different parts of the page that you can. That means the cover photo at the top, the profile pic, the address, contact details, services and so on. Basically, the more parts of this you fill out with good content, the better the page can connect with people who look at it.

We always recommend using a clear, friendly photo of your face for the profile pic rather than your logo, as it creates a more personal connection with followers. After all, it's called Facebook not Logobook!

Your Facebook posting strategy

We mentioned earlier that the best way to get people to engage with your content is to make your content more engaging. But what does that actually look like?

Here's the posting strategy we found works for us and our clients. This should be an ongoing strategic activity for your business.

Create engaging content

The most common way people will see you on Facebook in order to engage with you and your ideas is through the posts you make which appear in their feed.

When your posts get engagement, it's a sign that they are hitting the mark and your audience is responding. It shows you are gaining a reputation and traction in your community. It also gives you the ideal scenario to be able to then offer your paid services to this audience.

Remember – it's about them

Over and above all the other posting strategies we outline here, you must remember that you are publishing your posts to appeal to your *audience* – not to *you*. So forget the posts that have muscle charts or scientific explanations of how trigger points are formed. Other therapists might be interested in that, but it will go over the heads of most clients.

Instead, talk about the kinds of topics you would chat about with them in the less serious parts of treatment, or if you saw a client you like at the supermarket. You also know the kind of things they enjoy on Facebook itself from the research you've now done, and you should use the responses you receive as you go to adjust your message as well.

You're like any other publisher now, with your Facebook page being the equivalent of the old publisher's newspaper. You first of all need to keep your readers happy so they continue reading, and that allows you to raise your reputation, increase your influence, and reach your other goals from the relationship.

Post 10 times a week, or more
Only some of your followers see each post you put out, and if a post gets a good reaction from the first few viewers then Facebook will show it to more people. So you need to be putting out a reasonable amount of content in order for more people to have a chance to see it.

Use the rule of thirds
To ensure your content is reaching the various goals you have, split it into approximate thirds:

- *One third is purely for "engagement" or entertainment:* Use what you know of your audience and the other things they like on Facebook to put out photos and posts that align with their interests. Have fun! Support your brand message but keep it light and entertaining. A picture of a funny cat having a massage is gold here.

99

- *The next third is "about you"*: Get your face into your feed! And also include the business itself and your lifestyle (or parts of it) that align with your mission. For example, to support our clinic's mission of "Inspiring Exceptional Health", Elicia would post a photo of herself after running along the beach, with messy hair and red face. Being personal and authentic connects strongly with your community.

- *The final third is "promotional"*: Openly share bookings you have available, photos of products, or a special offer you might be running. You should keep these promotional posts quite simple and direct, not pushy but honest in their promotion. Posts that have a simple message like "we have availability next Thursday" or show your opening hours will often attract bookings once you have an engaged audience.

By starting with this balanced rule of thirds you can test and experiment to see what works for you as you find your balance between engaging your audience and creating the business outcomes you need.

Have daily themes

The idea with daily themes is *not* to make them public, but to give you a framework for yourself to make it easier to source your content and balance your message appropriately. Your daily themes should align with the rule of thirds and give you a more detailed structure for your content.

This is very straightforward: you simply decide on a topic or message you want to associate with each day of the week. You might decide that every Monday you will post something inspirational for the start of the week, Tuesday is about functional exercise, Wednesday shows a professional photo of you or a staff member, and so on.

Then, you create a set of folders on your computer that match each of the days and are labelled with the theme name. You can download content, especially images, into each of the folders so that when it comes time to schedule your content each week you have a bunch of material at your fingertips to put it together quickly and easily. You can even reuse this content every few weeks because many people who saw it last time won't see it again, and if they do they'll probably have forgotten it in the whirlwind of posts in their feed.

Be personal

Over and over again we see that the most popular posts on therapists' feeds are the ones that are most personal. This can start with simple things like getting your own face into photographs and sharing your passions and hobbies that your audience will be able to relate to.

Another aspect of this is vulnerability. Followers respond very well to stories where you are vulnerable enough to share your hardships or struggles, especially if you have a story of pushing through to overcome the challenges. These vulnerability stories make a break from the too-perfect vision of life we often see portrayed on social media, they create a more authentic connection between you and your audience, and they invite viewers to go deeper and be more honest themselves.

Whatever being personal looks like to you, ensure that there is a human face to your page and brand.

Schedule posts

An objection that sometimes comes up from people who don't use Facebook for business much yet is that it takes so much time to be on your computer or phone every day doing posts. The answer to this is to schedule your content.

On a Facebook business page you have the option when creating a post to have it appear in your business page feed at a scheduled time, rather than right then and there. There's a little dropdown next to the "publish" button as you're creating a post that allows you to very simply set the date and time you'd like the post to appear. (It does not work the same way on your personal posts.)

What this means is that you can sit down for an hour once a week and schedule out all your posts for the week, using the posting strategies we have outlined in this chapter.

Mix up the types of content you publish

So far we've looked at the *content* and how to strategically balance that for best impact. Also remember to mix up the *types* of posts you do, such as images, video, shares and plain text. In general, people respond most to video and photos, so they should be prominent in your mix, but include the others as well so that you've got a good mix.

(Facebook "Lives" are a specific type of video that is getting more engagement on Facebook than any other content at the moment, all other things being equal. Lives are so powerful at connecting that we've given them their own section a little later in the chapter, so that we can delve into them in more detail.)

Study your Insights

At the top of your business page there's a tab labelled "Insights" that contains some powerful statistics on your page and how your audience is interacting with your content. It's worth poking around in the Insights just to see what's there and to become familiar with the kinds of statistics available.

The simplest and most powerful statistics include:

- what time of day your followers are most active on Facebook
- their age and gender breakdown
- which of your recent posts has had the most engagement.

The statistics on post engagement are especially useful as you can recognise patterns and see what is working best to connect with your current audience. Once you can see the pattern of what works, you can do more of that!

Example social media posts

Keep experimenting

People change, and Facebook changes too, so you must constantly experiment and adjust to find what works best. For example, there was a time at our clinic when we had one of our reception staff scheduling our Facebook posts based on the strategy Elicia had created (which we've outlined above). At that time, Friday was our "inspirational post" day. Most of the time it would be a quote over a background pic. But one Friday, our receptionist had scheduled a photo of a shirtless Ryan Gosling with something like, "I'll be at the finish line with a bottle of wine and a puppy". Inspirational? Maybe. But we also had a strong rule about not sexualising the massage industry, so Elicia was shocked and a little worried… but the huge number of likes and shares it received helped "the occasional Ryan Gosling post" become part of our official strategy!

FACEBOOK LIVES

Live video on Facebook is such an important tool at the moment that we felt it needed its own section here! The purpose of live video as part of your strategy is to connect more fully with your clients, so in our four-part social strategy framework it is most often used within the "connection and engagement" phase.

How Facebook Lives work

A "Facebook Live" is live streaming video used as one of your post types within your publishing strategy. Being "live" means it works differently to the other content on your feed. Usually, you select in advance the video or image or other content that you will post, and you can check or edit it thoroughly before posting it. Live video streams immediately, so it works by showing your video to your audience at the actual time you are recording it.

The experience works like this: you type your video title in the box, then press the button to start the Live, it counts down 3, 2, 1 – and then you start talking, and people can watch you live.

Once you finish, you press the "end" button and the screen will ask you if you want to post the video to your page or discard it. If you post it to your page (and you should) it now behaves like a pre-recorded video would: people can continue to see it and comment, but it's obviously not actually "live" any more.

Why is live video so important? Lives reach more people than other types of content, plus the audience will connect and engage at a more personal level. Some of this is due to the way Facebook's algorithm works: it wants people to use live video more so it rewards the behaviour by giving it more reach. Plus people naturally engage more with them because they are a more natural, personal and authentic way to communicate.

Example Facebook Lives

How to create good-quality videos

A great advantage to using live video is that you don't need any special equipment. A modern smartphone is the only required tool, and the look and feel of your live video will be natural and unfiltered, which helps to connect you to your audience in a more authentic way.

This lack of post-production effects and studio editing is part of the charm and attraction of using live video. However, you still need to ensure that the people watching can see and hear you well enough to connect with your message, so here's a few tips for live video:

- Make sure your face is nicely lit, so that it looks smooth, without dark shadows.

- Use "Selfie Mode" on your phone so you can see your own face as you speak.

- If you are connected to Wi-Fi, ensure that it is a strong enough signal to support your live video, otherwise it gets pixely.

- Have your topic planned out and then speak from the heart – don't try to read a script, just trust yourself. You talk to clients all the time about these topics – you've got this.

- Get into a great state before you go live: listen to your fav song, get super grateful… whatever works for you.

- Speak for two to five minutes minimum, as it takes 30 to 60 seconds or so for Facebook to recognise that you're live and to let your audience know. If you get on and blurt it all out super quickly and finish, your audience will miss it.

- Remember to look at the camera not your own face on screen, so that your audience sees your eyes looking directly at them. The camera looks like a small black dot.

- Be consistent – do them regularly and don't get discouraged if no-one jumps on. Continue doing them anyway. People still see them once you have published them to your page.

CHAMPION SNAPSHOT: LISA ELWELL

Lisa is a remedial therapist from Perth who shared a powerful story at a recent client retreat of ours. She had been working on her marketing and recently completed a series of 30 Facebook Lives in 30 days. One of the other therapists in the room asked her how she had found the confidence to do them, and Lisa's reply was that she was *not* confident until she'd done the first 10 or more! Through the daily practice of this intense challenge Lisa grew her confidence and skills at presenting herself and her value.

How to write a CATCHY TITLE

When writing the title make it short, enticing, and use emojis and ALL CAPS to get more attention. Don't tell people exactly the info you will have in your Live but make sure they know the question you will be answering or the problem you will solve, so that the title makes the connection and opens that loop of "Oh, I definitely want to know that!" in your audience. Then they'll watch the Live and participate in order to find the answers they need.

For example, instead of "How to stretch at your desk" you could write:

*** THE THREE THINGS EVERY COMPUTER USER MUST DO IN THE AFTERNOON TO STAY ALERT 🤔 ***

What do I talk about?

The purpose of doing a live video for your audience is to educate or inform them in line with one of the topics on which you are an authority. But a live video on a social media platform like Facebook is a very light and entertaining way to educate people, so think less of a classroom teacher style and more of what it's like to talk to one of your friends when they ask you a question about what you do.

Facebook Lives should feel friendly and informal, and one of the huge secondary benefits to them is that your audience gets to see and hear you, notice your body language, pick up on your personality, and gets to know you more than in any of the other online content you produce.

For your topic, think in a similar way to what you do with blog posts or your other educational Facebook posts. Use topics that are in line with your authority areas.

It can also be very useful to write down the basic dot points of what you want to cover so that you have a framework to follow. Write them in large print on a piece of paper and stick it somewhere you can see it during the video but your audience can't. Don't simply read it, but use it as a prompt so that you don't forget your key points during the video.

How long should I speak for?

A live video is usually longer than a pre-recorded video would be, because it's less scripted and people come in and out, so you typically welcome them each as they arrive and may repeat certain key points a few times.

The way live video works on Facebook, people won't be watching live when you start the video. It takes 30 to 60 seconds or so for the first people to get the notification that you're on live and for them to join. Then more people will continue to join over the length of time you are speaking.

Spend the first minute or so on a basic intro and speaking casually about what you're doing or how the week has been. The idea is that people who watch this back on the replay will need to feel involved, but you don't want to use your best content too early or the people that arrive live will miss it.

As you progress into your content, you can continue to welcome new watchers and respond to questions and comments. At the start, this may feel like it interrupts your flow, but think of your Live more like you are speaking to a circle of friends – it's quite natural for people to cross talk and interrupt and still allow the main speaker to get their point across. It becomes more natural with practice.

A typical "live" video timeline might look like this:

0:00	Start; introduce yourself and make small talk
0:30	Start an intro to the topic
1:00	Point #1
3:00	Point #2
5:00	Point #3
6:00	Repeat all three points briefly
7:00	Finish

And of course, as with everything, see what length you are most comfortable with and what gets the most engagement with your audience.

FACEBOOK GROUPS

Facebook "groups" are another fabulous way to engage with more clients and gain recognition locally. Groups are a way for likeminded people to connect around a topic of interest using Facebook. Groups exist for hobbies, fans of TV shows, life experiences, sports clubs, support groups – basically anything. And almost every town, suburb and region has a community group where locals connect.

These groups are perfect for massage therapists as they allow you to connect with people who you know already have something in common... even if it's as simple as their postcode.

How Facebook groups work

Only personal profiles can join groups, so you must join as "you" not as your business. This is part of the power of groups, as members tend to have more conversations and connection in groups with other real people rather than business personas.

Because they are more personal, and due to the way Facebook's notification system works, people are more likely to see group posts than those from your business page, and they are even more likely to get a notification if you are also Facebook friends with them.

This means you should behave differently in groups than when you post from your business page. Get to know people in the group, answer questions, be part of the conversations. Become part of the community and people will begin to recognise your name and what you do. You could become the community hero, recognised because you regularly appear in the group. This is just like networking in real life, and it has long-term benefits as more people get to know you and remember you. If you're doing it well, you'll find people actually tag you in when the right kind of questions or topics come up. When they do, it's a sign that your message is getting through.

Because you can only post into the group from your personal profile, not your business page, if you do have an extremely awesome business post you want to put in the group you must "share" it in using your personal profile. Many groups have specific days when businesspeople are allowed to post promotionally. Always take advantage of this and post whenever you can, remembering to be respectful and follow the guidelines so you can continue to build a good reputation within the community.

"Courage starts with showing up and letting ourselves be seen."

Brené Brown

Client VIP groups

Once you have a reasonable number of clients you can consider creating a group specifically for your clients. It should be optional for them to join, but if you call it a "Client VIP Group" and put in last-minute appointment availabilities and special offers or similar, plenty of them will jump on board.

There are two main advantages to a group like this:

- More people will see the group posts for free, when compared with page followers not in the group.

- Your group posts are viewable only by the people in the group, so it's a great way to communicate special offers.

If you do set up a client Facebook group, treat it as communication with existing clients rather than reaching out to newbies. So your posting strategy can be quite different. You don't need to do as much of the broad engagement content. Instead, focus on bringing value to the group members so that they feel special for being part of it. For example, put unique videos or Lives in there, as well as sharing your offers.

FACEBOOK MESSENGER

The Messenger part of Facebook allows you to share chat messages with your Facebook friends. It's a simple tool but very flexible: as well as text, you can send images, emojis, audio, short videos, links, and of course funny GIFs.

The way Messenger is used now combines and replaces a lot of what people used to do on email and SMS, plus a whole lot more. A huge difference is the number of people who actually open and read these messages – in our experience, if we get 15% to 20% of our subscribers opening our emails we're doing well, whereas we see open rates of 95% and above with every Messenger message we send.

The best thing about Messenger is that it's simple and personal. Potential clients can contact you using Messenger very easily through your business page on Facebook, to ask about appointments or to touch base about other questions.

How Facebook Messenger works

So how do you make yourself open to messages?

Messenger is enabled by default on your Facebook business page, so you can monitor your page inbox if you're using the Facebook website, or install the Facebook Page Manager app to send and receive messages on your phone. You can also change the default button on your Facebook business page to say "send a message" (although "book now" is still preferred if you take online bookings).

If you want to take advantage of this growing communication channel, you can let people message you in a few other ways too:

- add the "send a message" button to the bottom of your paid Facebook adverts (see below) instead of sending people directly to your website or online bookings

- tell people to message you through your Facebook page for more info, when you do your content pieces

- add a Facebook Messenger chat box to your website so that people on your site can type a message directly to you.

A fantastic feature of Messenger that isn't utilised yet as much as it will be in the future is the ability to reach out to people who you have chatted with at any time, after the initial conversation. So if anyone ever asks a question or even just says hi, you can message them a month later letting them know you've had a last-minute cancellation that you can offer them if they're keen. And because so many people have the Messenger app on their phone, they will often get the message immediately and respond quickly.

This can be a great way to connect with clients who haven't been in for a while, to send reminders or link people to new blog posts or videos you've created that you know will be useful for them. It becomes an awesome tool for engaging and retaining clients, kind of like an email list but shorter and friendlier. And way cooler.

 ## USEFUL TOOL: ManyChat

A really cool development in this area that's still fairly new is what is known as a "Messenger bot". This is an automated sequence of messages that can be used to contact your audience or reply to questions automatically. Imagine that any Facebook message you get to your business inbox that has the word "appointment" in it anywhere gets an automatic reply sent with a link to your booking calendar. Cool, right? If you want to test it out, go to our website at www.massagechampions.com and enter the word "reader" in the chat box that pops up at the bottom right-hand side. You'll have fun, we promise!

ManyChat also includes tools to broadcast a single message to all your contacts, schedule messages in advance and track statistics for how many people read and click your messages. It's super cool, so if you're interested in using Messenger in a more powerful way take a look at their website: manychat.com

FACEBOOK PAID ADVERTISING

So far we've looked at how to use the community-building side of Facebook and the tools it has to promote yourself and your business for free. The next step is to look at Facebook and learn to use it as one of the most powerful paid advertising platforms available on the planet.

How Facebook paid advertising works

The reason Facebook advertising is so powerful is that it can be targeted to people according to demographics such as location, age, and interests. In other forms of advertising you pay to put your ad onto the platform and all the users see it. For example, an advert in a newspaper or a billboard on a highway shows your advert to everyone who is reading or passing by. You expect that your potential clients are present in the watching crowd, but the nature of newspapers and billboards is that you're paying for a stack of people to see your message when only a few of them are relevant.

Facebook advertising is the complete opposite of this. When you pay for an advertisement you get to choose who will see it. This means your message can be perfectly crafted for the target audience you have chosen for the ad. For example, if there is a marathon coming up near you and you know there are local runners who would benefit from a package that would carry them through pre-training and post-event treatments, you can target them. You can create an ad with a photo of a marathon runner with text that says "Entering the City to Surf Marathon? Massage can help with training and recovery AND it feels great!" A short example, but you get the idea... this advert can then be shown only to a specifically targeted audience who live within 20 kilometres of your clinic and have an interest in running. Bingo! The connection is made because the message matches the reader so perfectly, and you only pay for your advert to be seen by people who you have selected as relevant.

As you can see even from this simple example, Facebook is a very sophisticated tool for advertising. There are many ways to use it and the options change regularly, but luckily massage therapists can usually be very effective with just a few simple techniques.

A recipe for a great ad

For any ad to be effective it needs to have four parts that are all strong. When these four ingredients are all working together they form a complete circle that creates powerful results, whether that is engagement or bookings. If any of these factors is weak then the advert will cost more for any results it produces, or it may not produce any results at all.

The ingredients for a great ad are:

- offer

- image

- text

- targeting.

Let's have a look.

Offer

The first and most important ingredient is the offer that the advert holds. What we mean by this is the thing you are selling; we don't mean a "special offer" like "20% off" or "buy one, get one free" – in fact, we advise against those kinds of discounts in most cases. By "offer" we simply mean that you need to understand why people really buy what you do. In this sense it's not the service of massage or a specific treatment that you are selling, it's the outcomes or benefits of what you do.

People really want solutions to their problems or support reaching their goals, and they won't connect the word "massage" with what they want unless they already know what benefits it can give them or they have experienced it before and made that link themselves. Many people are not clear on the link between their underlying wants and the treatment "massage".

So what do you need to do? Look at your "offer" as being the core benefit to the person you want to treat. It's like that old adage of someone going into the hardware store to buy a drill. Do they actually want the drill? No. What they *really* want is a hole in their wall to hang their picture up. So the offer of "hang your pictures up easily and quickly" is better than "drills for sale".

What is your offer? It can change from ad to ad or over time, and you can have different offers for different audiences. But be sure you are clear on what it is and what the benefits will be to your audience when they come in for a treatment.

Image

The main purpose of the image in your advertisement is to gain attention. It needs to match your offer, and it should be bright, colourful, and have a person's face in it if possible. Facebook's interface itself is a sea of white and blue, so if you can get photos that have solid areas of a strikingly contrasting colour they stand out nicely. Try bright yellow, pink or green.

Also look at the content of the photo. Some pictures tell a little story and make you want to look at them. For example, one of the basic advert templates that we teach to many new therapists is what we call the "shocked" advert. It shows a picture of two people, the first whispering something to the second who has a look of extreme shock or surprise on their face. This style of photo makes you want to look at it, even if only briefly, because it subconsciously arouses curiosity. When this is the case, the image has done its job and the accompanying text can deliver a message. To match this image the message would be short, sharp and direct.

Something important to note on Facebook is that the image on your advert needs to be mostly made up of a photo or graphic – you can't have more than 20% of the image covered by text. This means you can have a caption or headline over part of the image but that's about it. For more detail you can use the text area of the advert or link through to a page on your website.

The small headline or caption over the image can be eye-catching and is important for grabbing attention, and it's even more important to make it look good because it is visually small.

USEFUL TOOL: CANVA.COM

A fabulous tool for editing your images to add text or logos on top is Canva.com, a very simple and free image editor which is available as a website or device app. One of the best features of Canva is that it has template sizes for all the major social media networks, including Facebook, so when you start a new image you can choose the "Facebook advert" template and it will make your ad the correct dimensions. You then add your image or select from one of the stock photos Canva has available (many for free) and add your text on top. Export it and it can be added to your Facebook advert like any other image.

Text

The text that goes with your advertisement (also called "copy") is the next part your audience will look at after your image catches

118

their eye, and the purpose of the copy is to better connect with them, communicate your offer with power, and encourage them to take the next steps.

This can be done in various ways, so it's important to experiment and use different techniques when creating your adverts. Start with something short, only a few sentences, and then test different styles of copy to discover what works best with your tribe. Be fun, then be more formal, then lighthearted – you'll find that there are themes or even individual words that resonate well with them.

Watch what other people do to springboard ideas for your own adverts. You can follow other massage therapists; as long as they are not local they are not direct competitors. Also follow other successful health professionals; for example, personal trainers, wellness coaches or nutritionists. By watching what other people do you get ideas for adverts to try.

Importantly, don't just copy the adverts word for word from other people. For starters, it's bad form, and as well as that you'll find that even the most successful advert doesn't work the same for everyone. For example, Jason is a client of ours from a little while ago who got fantastic traction with the "shocked" ad formula mentioned earlier. When he put that together while doing our program he used our template with almost no changes and got five bookings in 48 hours with only a $10 ad spend. Jason has gone on to consistently get good results from Facebook advertising for his business. However, other clients have found that the wording or imagery for that style of advert doesn't resonate with their tribe for some reason. This is why we suggest trying several different types of adverts and continuing to learn more about your tribe by doing more posting, research, and experimentation.

Sometimes people feel lost when it comes to how to write adverts that connect well with the audience and get results, especially on

Facebook – it's so busy and crowded that an advertisement really needs to hit home or it will be overlooked and ignored. So how do you ensure that your text copy always connects in a simple and powerful way? An easy method is to use the acronym PSOAS as you write your copy, which stands for:

- Problem

- Solution

- Outcome

- Action

- Stick.

Write about each step in this order and it provides a natural flow to your writing. Let's see how it works:

- **Problem:** Connect with your audience immediately by stating a specific problem you know they have and which you can solve. Write this in a way that connects with how they feel internally about the problem, as well as identifying the problem itself. For example, you could write problem statements like, "Finding it harder to recover from a long day of training since turning 40?" or, "Does it seem like you're spending all your time cooking and cleaning for your family in the school holidays?" They don't have to always be questions, but the idea is you connect with the audience at a level which lets them know that you know and understand who they are and their experience of life and the problem you're highlighting at a deeper level.

  One thing to be cautious of is that Facebook doesn't allow overly negative language, so you may need to be creative when it comes to wording the problem that you are connecting with.

It's quite common to have to rewrite tricky topics a handful of times before getting them passed.

- **Solution:** Offer the immediate, short-term solution to their problem; most commonly this is in the form of one of the services you provide and how it solves the problem stated in the first part. For example, you could say something like, "Post-event massage is shown to improve recovery time," or simply, "Massage can help!"

- **Outcome:** The outcome follows on from the solution and extends that idea into the long-term benefits or results that can be attained. Focus on what's in it for the reader and ask yourself what it means for them when they have the solution to their problem. For example, "Get back to training like you're 20 again", or, "Show your team mates you've still got what it takes", or in another scenario, "Get back to being the Mum you know you want to be as you're filled with calm and confidence".

- **Action:** This is where we point to the next step and encourage the reader to book in, or click through for more information. For simple adverts connecting with an audience familiar with you it's possible to link directly to your online booking calendar and get good results from that. For cooler audiences or those unfamiliar with your modality as a solution to their problem, you may need to link to your website for more information (and from there link to the booking calendar).

    Examples of this are quite simple and should be direct and easy to understand, like "Click now to book" or "Save time, book online", followed by the website or booking link. The button that goes beneath your advert is added as you're creating the advert, and should be set to go to the same link.

- **Stick:** The stick is a little extra nudge to encourage the reader to take action now rather than later. This can range from "Bookings available this Thursday" to "Offer ends midnight tonight". See how the use of a timeframe gives the sense of urgency? This encourages people to take action now rather than wait (and then most likely forget).

Using harsh or restrictive "sticks" can seem forced if it is done too often, so keep most of them gentle or leave a stick off altogether if appropriate.

So the example copy here, put all together, would read like something like this:

Finding it harder to recover from a long day of training since turning 40?

MASSAGE is shown to improve recovery time!

Feel GREAT and get back to training like you're 20 again

Save time BOOK ONLINE: www.yoursite.com

Only a few places left this week…

Along with a colourful image of a sportsperson stretching, this would be a great advert to test along with others that are simpler and more direct.

Write your own text copy using the PSOAS method and experience how much easier this framework makes it to write words that truly connect with your audience.

Targeting your ads

Targeting your advert controls who sees it. There are many options for this in Facebook, from simply paying so that more of your likers and followers see your posts, through to extremely detailed targeting that can be based on demographics and interests. You could, for example, show an ad only to men aged in their 40s who have primary-school-aged children, an interest in running, live within 15 kilometres of your clinic *and* have visited your website in the last 30 days.

Targeting is where the true magic of Facebook lies, because this is what allows you to send the right message to the right person so perfectly. This is incredibly powerful once you have clarity on your niche: who it is you are serving and what you do for them.

Most often the trick with targeting your niche is in finding the balance between specificity and size. The targeted audience must be specific enough to respond to your advert (because the advert itself is specifically designed for them) while still being broad enough to contain enough people to achieve many bookings and support your business long term.

When you target people with specific traits on Facebook you can experiment with the message and offer you send them to see what gets the best reaction. This is ongoing research and naturally leads to you finding the most effective messages that connect you with your audience.

Being seen by more people

One option for targeting is to simply show your advert to people who follow your page, or to those people plus their Facebook friends. If you've got a reasonable size following of at least a few hundred people and you know they are a good tribe that connects with you, this can be an excellent tactic for ads that promote direct bookings. Your followers already know who you are, so it's an easy group to market to.

Boosting a post

You can target your existing followers with any type of advert, but the absolute simplest way to advertise on Facebook and the way most people first wet their feet is by boosting a post. You've probably noticed the handy blue "boost" button that sits directly beneath your posts when you are looking at your own business page feed.

Boosting a post is an example of wanting a simple outcome from what you're doing – basically you just want more people to see the post you're putting out. To test this out, choose one of your recent posts or create a new one that you want to use as an advertisement. Click the "boost" button and follow the prompts.

Boosting in this way gives you a simpler set of options to select from, but otherwise is basically the same as creating a "post engagement" style advert from within the advert manager. This is why it can be a good place to start before stepping into the next level of advertising.

Boost sparingly. It's a great way to get content out to a wider audience, which is perfect if that aligns with your goals. Don't bother boosting posts that don't have a specific purpose or are simply part of your "engagement" content. On the other hand, if you want to get a booking filled for a cancellation you've had for the next day, you can do a post along the lines of, "A spot has just become available tomorrow afternoon! Book in now", and then boost that for the afternoon.

Also, don't be fooled by Facebook popping up and suggesting to you things like "page admins have boosted posts like this one" – Facebook obviously wants you to spend more money, but it's only worth it if it has a benefit towards you reaching your business goals.

Targeting new clients

When you boost an advertisement to your existing audience it's like scooping the net into your audience and getting bookings from the people who are there. Targeting new clients with ads grows your audience and attracts new people into your tribe.

When you create an advertisement for new people your message must speak to them and their problems first before you start offering your treatments as the solution. This is because many of them will not have heard of you before and may not even be aware of the benefits of massage or your specific modality.

Advertising to new clients is where the copywriting framework PSOAS becomes really useful, as the flow of your text creates a connection based on a problem that the reader is currently experiencing.

When it comes to the point of selecting the audience who will see your advert, there are two sets of options on the page. First is general demographics like age, gender and location. Second is a box titled "interests", where you can add interests or behaviours that Facebook knows about its audience. This is where you can add interests like "football", "Chef Pete Evans" or the "Brisbane Marathon". The same box also lets you type in attributes like "parents with young children" or "away from home".

If you were following along earlier when we looked at researching your audience, you will have looked at a bunch of people that you know are your target audience already and explored the common interests they have. This is where targeting can be really effective as you can create an advertising message specifically for a type of audience member and then target them so that the only people who see the advert are the ones you know are most likely to respond.

Your self-selected audience

The third type of audience to look at is one that you define from a list of people that you provide. This can happen in a few different ways.

Firstly, you can upload a spreadsheet list of your clients into Facebook to create an audience. Facebook checks their email address, phone number and name, and tries to match the details you have supplied with people it knows about on Facebook. Not everyone uses their main email address for their Facebook account so it can't always find the entire list, but usually about 80% of your uploaded people will be matched.

Why is this powerful? This is especially useful for targeting your existing or past clients with re-engagement campaigns, and it means you can use data that you have on your clients outside of Facebook to decide who will see the ads. For example, if you can produce a report from your booking software of all your clients who have not seen you in the last six months, you could then put that list into Facebook and create an offer that says, "We haven't seen you in a while", with a bonus to encourage them to book in again. It's much easier to re-engage a past client because they have already experienced who you are and are more likely to come back in.

You can also set up a tracking pixel on your website so that Facebook can track the people who visit, and you can then make a target audience for your advert based on people who have either visited any part of the site or a specific page. You can't actually see a list of their names but Facebook keeps track behind the scenes and lets you send adverts directly to that audience. This is super cool for creating what we call a "self-selected" audience. For example, when you write a blog post on a particular topic, like "5 stretches marathon runners can do to reduce muscle soreness", you can be fairly sure that only people interested in that topic will click through to your website to read it. They will get tracked by the Facebook pixel, and then you can run something like a "Marathon Package" as an advert to only those people.

Facebook also lets you create a "Lookalike" audience based on other audiences you've created. You select the "seed" audience that you want to expand and Facebook looks at all the common traits it sees about them and then matches more people that it sees would fit. Using lookalike audiences in this way can get amazing results if your seed audience is at least a few hundred people who fit your ideal client well.

 ## EXERCISE: TEST AND MEASURE

So much of the success of your advertising will come from your ability to test and measure what is working quickly and efficiently, and being responsive with changes and adjustments to get the best results. So set yourself the task of creating one advert per week for the next month – or if you want to see faster growth, do four per week for the month. Spend money on each one and you'll start to see the statistics that show you what is working and what isn't.

INSTAGRAM

Instagram is the only other social media we're going to discuss in detail here, because it's the only place besides Facebook that we see therapists using to regularly get bookings. There are others that might work and you can look at them if you know your audience uses them regularly, but for most people Facebook is number one and Instagram is an optional number two, and the rest don't matter.

Instagram vs Facebook

Instagram is similar in many ways to Facebook, and the basic posting strategy that we've shown you above will work almost the same way as you use your content topics to grow your audience and reputation. But to get the most out of Instagram you need to understand that it is different to Facebook in a few important ways:

- It's very visual – all posts need to be either an image or a video, and most don't have much text that goes with them.

- You follow your friends and other people on Instagram to see their pictures, but it's more open and public and the look and feel is simpler.

- You can't use links in your post descriptions, which means you have to simply direct people to your website or your main bio link if you want them to book somewhere.

- Instagram is also used mainly as an app from your phone, with the idea that you're sharing shots you are taking right now wherever you are. (But in reality many of the photos are highly staged or manipulated, and then coloured filters and edits are applied in the Instagram software before it goes live.)

In fact, if you haven't used Instagram much before, one of the first things you'll notice is that people here love beautiful images. The posts that are the most beautiful get the most likes, which means that it works wonders for people in businesses that sell beautiful products. Interior design, models, fashion and food all do well on this platform, and to make it work as a massage therapist you'll need to take great photos of your room or yourself.

You can use pre-edited images like those you might create for Facebook, but to put them onto Instagram you have to send them to yourself on your phone, save them to your photo library or camera roll, and add them into Insta that way.

Using #hashtags

Use #hashtags to get new followers on Instagram. By adding a hashtag to a post you essentially categorise the post with that word. People can click the hashtagged word on their phone to see other posts tagged with the same word, so in this way users explore topics they're interested in. For example, the Great Ocean Road marathon might have the hashtag #gormarathon and then every post with that same hashtag might be seen by people who are interested in the event.

To make your posts get seen by more people you should add 20 to 30 hashtags to each one, and here's a hot tip: add the hashtags as the first comment on your own image rather than in the main description. This still works the same way for people finding the image, but it means your image description text isn't messed up with all those #s.

How do you know what hashtags to use? Look at what your audience is already searching for and sharing about, and then always include locally relevant words as well... don't just use #massage. It might take some getting used to, but if you jump in and start using Instagram regularly you'll see how other people are doing it and what works.

Posting on Instagram

You can use a very simple posting strategy for Instagram, and luckily the content can be recycled into Facebook quite easily in most cases. Post a picture every day and rotate between the

"3 Cs" for this: credibility, character and connection. So, a post that shows your credibility and authority, a post that shows your character and leadership, and a post that gives a personal connection. Cycle through these, and once or twice a week add in the fourth "C" of call to action, and give people a reason to call you or book online. This can be done using the same kind of post we looked at for Facebook, but with more emphasis on the image and less text.

USING VIDEO IN YOUR ONLINE CONTENT

Your audience can see you, hear you and get a feel for your body language and mannerisms when they watch you on video. This builds a very high level of trust and authenticity, as well as making it an excellent way to communicate.

There are a number of ways to include video in your online content.

Social media video

We've already looked at Facebook Live video earlier in this chapter, a powerful way to use video on social media that gets great reach on that platform right now. You can also, of course, pre-record your video for social media. Any modern smartphone gives you the ability to shoot, edit and publish videos of a fantastic quality that are certainly suitable for your marketing needs.

In general, if your video is for social media, you should choose to make more videos, more often, rather than spending too much time on making them look professional. This is because on Facebook or Instagram, a video only stays around as content for a short time, so if you spend too long putting it together you won't get a good return on your time.

Also on social, video length is usually very short. Instagram has a limit of one minute for videos, and although Facebook doesn't have a restriction like that, if you are pre-recording and editing videos, aim to keep them short and punchy. Because these are more organised than your live videos they will usually get to the point quicker, and often the most popular videos are only one to three minutes in length. Say what you will be talking about or what problem you are about to solve right at the start of the video, in the first 10 seconds, so that people are hooked to watch the rest if it's a topic that interests them.

Here's some things you can do on video for your social media audience:

- talk about a topic you are expert in – educate

- show a technique

- show a product

- tour your clinic or room

- demonstrate stretches or aftercare

- share something from your life

- share something inspirational or motivational

- be creative.

Also remember that, like with everything else, it's the message that is most important here. If your message or offer is strong, the video only needs to be good enough quality to convey that message without causing any communication hurdles. Then your viewers will connect with what you are saying rather than giving the video itself a second thought.

Case studies

Most massage associations will allow you to do case studies, although not all, so it's important to check. If you are able to use them, great! They are a valuable way to build trust with people who haven't met you yet. Always get written permission and consent from the client and tell them where you will be publishing it – this includes consent to use their name and age publicly.

When you do a case study video, it's good to have it like a casual conversation: where were they before you started working together, what did they come in for, what did you do with them, what's been the difference for them since?

It's often good to set this up in your treatment room, so long as you have great lighting or can use some camera lights to brighten it up. It can be a 30-second vid going over all of the above briefly, or it can be a 10- to 20-minute video. If it's a really great case study, we would suggest the longer format. Aim to have one to five of these that you plan to do over a few months.

Once you have the footage, you can add subtitles to it using your video editing software, which is worth the time investment because it will help you reach far more people. Subtitles get your message across even if the watcher has their sound turned off, which is very common on mobile phones. If you want to get super fancy with it, you can use Fiverr.com and get your logo put into a video format for around $10 in a few days and add this to the end of your videos.

CHAPTER 8

BUILDING AN AWESOME WEBSITE

BOOSTING YOUR ONLINE VISIBILITY

A website is a powerful tool in your marketing toolkit, for three important reasons.

Firstly, your website becomes a central hub for your content, allowing you to publish articles and videos and show your services – because it is by publishing relevant, popular content that you will become better known for your core messages and will have an impact on your community beyond just one-to-one treatments. This then has a doubly powerful impact because of the way you can track who views or interacts with this content, and then use that information to advertise and market directly to the people who are showing the most interest.

Secondly, a website will help you get found in a Google search. And people who are searching for "massage in *Your Suburb*" are always great leads because they already have what we call "intent to buy", in that they already know they want a massage and are looking for the right person to go and see. If your website appears before them and ticks all the boxes, they are very likely to make a booking there and then. Gold! (Although a website by itself is actually no guarantee you will appear well in the free search results, it is a vital step, and we'll look at some of the ways you can help the site to appear in free search, as well as paying to get there.)

Thirdly, a website is the most common place for people to do simple research on who you are. This means that it acts like rocket fuel to your other marketing. For example, if someone sees your sign as they drive past, or notices a post on Facebook, or even if they're referred by a friend, often the first thing they will do if they are thinking of booking in is Google your website and take a look. If your website looks professional and friendly and ticks the other boxes that they need, they'll continue through the funnel to book in with you.

We've met some therapists who clearly want a website when they first start up. Along with business cards and a massage table it can be seen as one of the staples of starting a new business. However, we don't believe this is the best option. It may seem like a strange point of view given that James ran a digital agency for 13 years and one of his staples across that time was building websites for small businesses. But what James learnt over that time is that yes, a website is a powerful tool, but it is not the first tool you need.

Instead of spending weeks of time or thousands of dollars building your website right at the start, it's much easier to start with a Facebook page and a phone number, and get a few clients coming through first. This way you will learn what types of services they like, what questions they always ask, and how to speak their language. You can then use what you learn to create your website a few months down the track. The more you understand your audience, the better the site will connect.

You can also start with a simple one-page website that has all the basic information you need, and expand out to more pages as you move forward.

WHAT DO I PUT ON MY WEBSITE?

The main purpose of a website is to create connection with your audience and encourage them to click through and book your services. Remember the marketing funnel we looked at in chapter 6? A website usually sits squarely in the middle of your funnel, and acts as the landing point for a lot of your top-of-funnel campaigns.

What this means is that different types of people end up on your website. Some will know you very well already and may even be current clients, while others might never have heard of you before but have just Googled for your service in the area. Your homepage should cater to the different needs of this range of viewers.

There are four basic things your website needs to do, whether it is a single-page site or is more developed with multiple pages and content. The four things your site needs are:

- who you are

- what you do

- why they should choose you

- how to book in.

These can be arranged in various ways to fit the look and feel you are creating, but we have included over the page a diagram of what an ideal homepage layout would look like, with all the pieces of content in place. By having all of these items present we are meeting the needs of different site visitors and the different questions they will have in mind. This structure also means that your site content flows in a way that is like telling a story, so that people find it natural and easy to follow what is being presented.

Let's have a look at each of these.

Who you are

Notice that this is the very first thing on the list, because believe it or not this is the most important. Potential clients need a connection with you and your business before they will look at your services.

Connecting happens in two ways on your website.

Your brand

First, the look and feel of the design needs to show the viewer the kind of business you are and the type of people you work with. In marketing terms we call this your "brand". Your brand includes your logo and business name, and also the consistent visual style you put out into the world. All your visuals add together to give an incredible amount of information about you before the viewer even reads a word.

You probably already know about this unconsciously. Imagine the sort of photography, colours and fonts you might see on two extremely different therapist websites. For example, a sports therapist site will look very different to a crystal healer. The sports site might have active images of people running, use strong red or blue highlights, and have bold, strong fonts. In contrast, a crystal healer will often use soft images, pale purples or greens, and thinner or more flowing fonts. It is natural to have these differences if each design is doing its job right, because each will appeal to the kind of clients that therapist wants to work with and can help the best.

Example home page

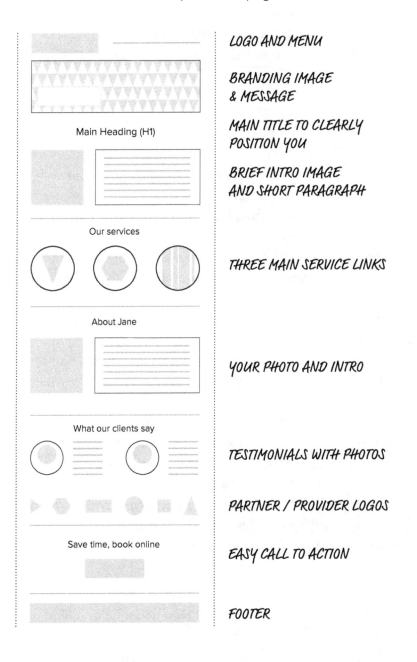

LOGO AND MENU

BRANDING IMAGE & MESSAGE

MAIN TITLE TO CLEARLY POSITION YOU

BRIEF INTRO IMAGE AND SHORT PARAGRAPH

Main Heading (H1)

Our services

THREE MAIN SERVICE LINKS

About Jane

YOUR PHOTO AND INTRO

What our clients say

TESTIMONIALS WITH PHOTOS

PARTNER / PROVIDER LOGOS

Save time, book online

EASY CALL TO ACTION

Studies show that it takes only about 50 milliseconds (that's 0.05 seconds) for viewers to decide whether they like your site or not, and only a few seconds more will determine whether they stay or leave. So it is vital your design connects strongly with your ideal audience.

Your face

The second way you need to show who you are is more personal.

Potential clients need to see you are authentic and professional. They want to get to know you even just a little bit, so that they can connect with you as a human, not just as a service. So somewhere on your homepage you should have a photo of you with an introduction next to it.

The photo should be professional and friendly. It doesn't have to be taken on a fancy camera or by a professional, although you can do that if you want to. However, even if you're taking it with a smartphone, make sure you're looking smart and your face is clear and bright. If you have a work uniform, wear it for the photo.

For the introduction wording that goes with it, we love to see therapists start with, "Hi, I'm James. I am passionate about ..." Fill in your own name and use your current passion for improving your clients' health to introduce who you are. This then frames the rest of your story so that readers can see what is in it for them.

Your homepage should have only one or two short paragraphs about you, and a link to your "about" page once you have one. That "about" page will contain a longer version of the same story: again, frame it with why you are passionate to help your clients right now, to put the relevance to your readers right up front.

What you do

The word "massage" is very well known. When it is combined with images or other words, most people will understand what it is that you do in a practical sense. But not everyone knows the benefits of massage, what it achieves, or what the different modalities mean. Yet we still see therapists getting stuck using technical or practical language rather than speaking in the language of the client.

Describing your services is a classic example. We quite often see things like, "Remedial Massage is a technique using physical manipulation to increase blood flow and release trigger points". While this may technically be true, it's not what a reader will want to hear about at the start.

Remember, some of the people on your website might not have ever had a massage before. Or maybe they've had a relaxation or a sports massage and you're using a technique they haven't heard of before, and they're wondering what it will be like and if it's going to help them. So instead of using those technical words, focus on the benefits of what you do. Think about "what's in it for them".

A better example might read, "Remedial Massage helps your tight muscles feel looser, improves flexibility, and enables you to recover from muscle injuries more quickly. Plus it leaves you feeling great!"

Obviously this is a very simple example. It's fine to go into more detail, but remember to start with the benefits. This gives your potential client a reason to continue to read the rest of the detail if they want to.

On your site there are two main places where you'll be talking specifically about what you do.

Headline

The headline at the top of your homepage sets the context for the entire site and should be a simple, clear introduction to what you do. It's the first piece of text most people will read on your site. It's usually short, only a handful of words, using a large font.

You can create a simple and powerful headline by breaking it into two parts to make it really easy. Start with the word "massage" if your modality can be described as that. This is good for Google as well as people. If you can't use massage, try to use simple words for your technique that people will understand without having to be told what it is. Then include either a benefit or a target audience in there for the second part. For example, your title might say "Massage to help sports injury recovery". This includes the technique ("Massage") and the benefit ("to help sports injury recovery"). Alternately you could say "Massage for athletes", which is including a target audience instead. "Massage for Athletes in Richmond" could be even better, as it tightens the target audience even more clearly.

Of course you can be more creative with your headline if you wish; simply keep in mind the purpose and context.

Your services

There will be a place on your homepage somewhere beneath the title that shows your services. We recommend limiting this to only three or four of your most popular or important services to keep it simple, and having an image with each one as well as the title. By making this visual, your site visitors can quickly see a very simple overview of what you do without concentrating on reading.

You can then have a separate page that goes into more detail, or have a little more beneath the services if you have only a single page. It's okay to have some detail, but it should be like a hierarchy

– very clear and simple at the top, with more detail beneath or on another page for those who want it.

Whether your service descriptions are long or short, no matter where they are you should still always focus on the benefits first before the technique or other details.

Why they should choose you

There are several practical things people need to know to book in with you. They are:

- where you are located

- what times you are available

- if you can help them.

The first two are easy enough to show with some text near the top of the page, so that it's visible without having to scroll far or read through a slab of details.

Showing that you can help them comes partly from your "what you do" content, and once those simple boxes are ticked, the biggest thing you need to create to get your readers to take the next step is... trust. When your site visitors trust you, they feel comfortable that you are professional and that they will be cared for appropriately when they visit. They have enough certainty in you and your services to overcome the inertia they will have around booking in for the first time.

So how do you show people that you are trustworthy?

The look and feel of your logo, website, and the language you use is the first thing. As we established earlier, viewers make snap judgements very quickly based on the visual appeal of your site. So when your site looks professional and clean and well designed, you can show you are trustworthy by *looking* trustworthy.

If you have won any awards or received specialised training or have decades of experience, these kind of attributes also build your authority and encourage people to trust you. They are most appropriate to mention in the section that is about you personally.

Testimonials and case studies are another fantastic trust builder. Even a single sentence from one or two of your clients, with their photos, shows that you have existing happy and loyal clients – this is what we call "social proof" that you are trustworthy.

A case study might be a more in-depth article or interview, or a video. You would publish this in the blog area of your website and link to it through social media, so that more people see it and it raises trust even with people who haven't been to your website yet.

Another simple way to build even more trust is with a row of formal logos from your suppliers or partners. For example, this could include organisations you are a member of, like your association or a chamber of commerce, or suppliers, like your oil or hot stones. Having three or four logos in a row shows that you are a professional who is connected with other businesses. You should keep this visually subtle because a row of colourful logos can distract from your own brand. But when managed gracefully, this is an excellent way to leverage from your relationship with other brands in order to enhance your own.

How to book

The main purpose of your website is to encourage people to book in, yet many times this focus is not reflected in the design.

If you have online bookings, you should have the link to this in several places. Some people will already want to book in the moment they arrive on your homepage. Others may not have heard of you before and they will need to experience some of your content first before they book in.

Whatever the client's journey through your website, you want to make sure they have an easy time booking in when they are ready for that step. Some of the places to put your booking button are:

- in the main top menu, ideally with a box around it or as a button so that it stands out from the other menu items

- as a button near the top of the homepage

- at the bottom of your homepage

- at the bottom of your services pages (if you have them) so that after someone has read about what you do they can easily click the button to book

- on your contact page, and every place you have your other contact information.

Where possible, the booking buttons should have space around them, top and bottom, and be centred on the page where that fits in the design. The space around the button makes it stand out.

If you don't have online bookings available yet, you should still place your preferred contact details on the homepage and at the bottom of the relevant services pages so people know the best way to take the next steps.

HOW DO I BUILD MY SITE?

There are basically two ways to create a website: either build it yourself or get a professional to build it for you. Thankfully, the practical side of building your own website can be very easy with the tools available online these days. You can go to sites like squarespace.com, wix.com or wordpress.com and sign up for an easy website builder for about $10 to $25 per month.

These sites let you select from hundreds of "themes", which are basically predesigned templates of a site, each with their own style to suit different purposes. When you choose a theme you like, you then fill it with your own photos and words to create your own website.

Squarespace and Wix both have drag-and-drop editors to make it really easy when you log in to edit your site. They also have plenty of video tutorials and email support to help guide you through the practicalities of the process.

WordPress is a little different – it's a more flexible platform which can be configured in many different ways. By default it doesn't have a drag-and-drop editor, but many of the themes you can select have an editor that comes with them, so once you choose one of them WordPress can be just as easy to use as any other system.

Many local web designers use WordPress because it has so many options, so you may find that if you're working with someone like that they will require you to use it. That's good – it means you and your designer can both edit your site and you can get help with anything specific that needs to be added or changed.

If you do choose to save yourself the time and effort and get someone to build your entire site for you, you can use the basic content outline we looked at earlier in the chapter to help guide the design and ensure your site has what you need to make it work well as a marketing tool.

There are some large companies that design and build websites, but unless you have a larger budget you will most likely find it easier to touch base with a local web designer to work with you on a more personal level. It can be hard to find a balance between skill level and price and it varies widely, but expect to pay anywhere from $1000 to $5000 for a professional website design.

A good web designer will give you advice and guide you through the process as they create your site for you. Before you start, look at the portfolio of the designer to check that they have created designs in a style that you like, and in similar industries.

CHAMPION SNAPSHOT: ANNE I'ANSON

Anne is a successful massage therapist who told us she was "afraid of technology" when we first met. She knew this held her back because she was stuck doing all her bookings by hand and was very limited in her marketing as she avoided anything online.

As we worked with Anne she took control of her mindset and worked through her tech challenges. She learnt what she needed to in order to build her very own website, and the best thing for her was the feeling of pride she had when it was complete and the first bookings from it came in. She proved that a simple, effective site is a major asset and it was worth the effort to create one.

CHAPTER 9

MAKING THE MOST OF GOOGLE

Google is the world's most popular search engine, and if someone is looking for a massage it's very common for them to search Google to find their local options. If your website or other online listings appear well in the search results then more people will see you when they are searching.

The great thing about Google is that active searchers have a powerful "intent", meaning they are looking for a solution to a specific problem they have right now. If you appear in front of them at this point it's often a smooth and easy path for them to join the dots and become a client. This is one of the "low-hanging fruit" opportunities online that can be a massive asset for the businesses that do appear high up in the results. But it's not necessarily easy to get there, so let's look at some of the simple things you can do to help.

GOOGLE MAPS

Google Maps is the most incredible free tool to appear in Google search. It's designed so that when someone is searching Google for a service in a location, it shows a map right there on the search results page, with the relevant local businesses shown as pins.

If you've got a phonebook listing or have been practising from your address for a while, chances are Google already has a free listing for you at your location. As well as showing on Google Maps, your listing appears in what Google calls "Google My Business", which is the main account used to control your business listing in Maps and a few other Google services. You can find out if you have a listing already simply by searching in Google Maps for your business name in your suburb. You will appear if Google already has you listed, and you can click a link to verify you are the owner.

If your business is not already there, you can select the option to add your business as a new entry and fill out a form to have your listing added.

Once you have control of your listing, fill in as much detail as you can. Add your business name, description, photos, everything. Adding more details gives you a better chance of appearing higher in search results, as well as making your listing more attractive to viewers.

What if you are mobile? Or work from home and don't want your address public?

That's okay – in both cases, you can set a suburb or postcode for Google Maps to use, so it will show your listing when someone searches in the right area, but viewers won't get the specific address of your location.

EXERCISE: REVIEW YOUR GOOGLE MAPS LISTING

If you haven't claimed your Google Maps listing yet, or it has only the basic information, this task should be at the top of your list! It's free and can get you immediate clients if they are searching in your area.

Check that your listing exists, and review it to ensure it is as complete as possible.

PAID ADVERTISING USING GOOGLE ADWORDS

"AdWords" is the name of Google's paid advertising service, and it can be a godsend to massage therapists. Basically, paying for AdWords means your website doesn't need to appear naturally in the search results. It can be notoriously difficult to appear in the free listings under searches like "massage in *Your Suburb*", and while we'll have a look at some tactics for doing just that below, it is a much simpler solution to pay for it.

Why is it so powerful to appear in search results at all? Remember that when someone is searching they already have that "intent to buy", which means they are more likely to book in compared to, for example, just seeing an ad in a newspaper. Conducting an online search means they already know they want to use your service.

How Google AdWords works

With AdWords, you can place a short text advert at the top or side of the search results in Google. You get to choose what searches (also known as "keywords") your website will appear under.

And the best thing is, you only pay for the advert when someone clicks it. That makes it a very economical activity for the top of your funnel, although the cost per click will vary depending on how many other therapists are advertising in your area under the same keywords. Usually a click will cost anywhere from $1 to $5, and you set your own budget for each day so usually a few dollars a day is a good place to start so that you can get at least a couple of people clicking through. You will need to track how many of these clicks turn into bookings to see whether or not it is working for you.

Then you write your ad. The format of the advert itself is restricted to a title and two lines of text beneath it, which are all limited by how many characters of text you can fit on them, so sometimes writing a meaningful advert that conveys your message can be challenging.

Set the link for your advert to go to the homepage of your website, or a specific service page if you have one that matches the relevant search term. You can also set your advert up to have a phone number as a call to action instead of the link if you don't have a website yet, but it's more common for people to click an ad rather than call, so use a link if you can.

Some of the therapists we work with get the majority of their new clients from AdWords, so it is definitely worth experimenting with.

AdWords Express

One important thing to note is that AdWords Express is a simpler version of the main AdWords. The Express version has the same outcomes and puts the ads in the same places, but is much easier to set up. You start by selecting the main keywords you want your advert to appear under – use the word "massage" and your suburb name for a start – and then the system will suggest other keywords that are similar.

SEO: THE SECRET TO SUCCESS ON GOOGLE

SEO stands for "search engine optimisation", and basically covers all the things you do to your website to help it appear higher up in search engine results. The reason so many people want to appear high up in Google is because it's a free way of getting in front of people who are searching for your services.

And yes, it's free in that you don't pay a fee to Google to appear there – unlike Google AdWords, which is the paid advertising service. But being well placed in free search results can be a lot of hard work, and there are people who will charge you thousands of dollars to help you appear at or near the top of these free listings.

So how can you help your website appear at the beginning of the free search results as easily as possible? The first thing to understand is that there are no guarantees when it comes to appearing well. When you look at how Google works you will understand why. When someone with a sore hip searches for a therapist, Google compares every web page in the entire world, billions of pages, and tries to deliver the single page at the top of the list that is most relevant to the query.

When deciding who goes to the top of the list, Google looks at two things. It interprets the content on your site to make sure you are answering the searcher's query. Then it looks at the "authority" of your site, which is basically a measure of how professional you and your site are.

So to improve your chance of getting to the top of Google, you need to work on both your content and authority. (Also note that by far the biggest and most important search engine is Google, but there are others. The methods used here work for Google and the rest too, for the most part.)

The content

For every page on your site, including your homepage, you should use the content on the page to show Google what the page is about. You do this by selecting what "keywords" you want your site to appear for. A keyword is basically the words or phrase that people will use when searching for you in Google. Usually the most beneficial for massage is "massage in *Your Suburb*".

So how do you target this keyword phrase? Simply ensure that you mention it in prominent places in the content of the page. This includes the written text, the descriptions for photos and the menu items. But the most important areas are the main headline on the page and the "SEO title" for the page, which your editing screen should give you access to. Think about it logically. If the headline for a page has the keywords in it, chances are the page is "about" that topic, and that's what Google wants to deliver to people searching.

It's also important that your pages have content that Google can "see" and understand. The words written on a page should always be written into a text area so that Google can access them. If not – for example, if your wording is saved into an image and then placed on your page – Google can't access those words.

You should have about 300 words minimum on any page that you want to appear well, as any less than that and it becomes too "thin" for Google to understand properly and therefore it won't rank well. This can seem like a lot sometimes, but it works best if it's split among several sections on the page, and anywhere with a large text block should be broken up with subheadings, dot points or images so it's easier to look at.

If your content is written with your readers in mind you'll find you naturally have your keywords and variations of the same spread throughout. You can tidy it up to include a handful of mentions of your keywords if they didn't make it into the first draft.

But when you're adjusting your content be careful not to overdo it. Google gets suspicious of people trying to "stuff" keywords in simply to appear well for topics or keywords that their site might not be 100% relevant for. So you should always write for people first, using natural language and writing about authentic topics that your tribe will be interested in. This will naturally use a lot of your keywords anyway and satisfies Google's scepticism.

And forgive us as we get just a little bit technical for a second, but this is important. Google only reads the code behind the scenes of your page and won't "see" the look of your page the same way human eyes do. For this reason, your code needs to be organised in a way that helps Google understand your content better.

The simplest thing to focus on – without getting a degree in IT – is that your headings are actually marked as headings in the code. This is actually pretty easy: when you use the content area editor dropdown to make something a "heading 1" or "heading 2", you're actually defining how important that heading is in the code, so Google recognises it as more important. This is different to a piece of paragraph text that has been made large and bold and looks like a heading to everybody else. Google sees them differently. So, make sure you get the geek stuff right as well – it's important for your search engine rankings.

Site authority

There are quite often multiple pages that compete for keywords by having similar quality content on their site. When this is the case, how does Google tell which page should appear first? This is where your site's authority score comes in. Google basically gives every site on the internet an authority score between 1 and 100, depending on how important or authoritative it thinks your site is.

Sites like Wikipedia and Microsoft.com get the ultimate score of 100, whereas unknown small business sites that have just launched will be a 1. Most sites end up somewhere between about 5 and 20 without trying too hard, once they've been around and active for a few months.

In simple terms, the higher your authority number, the higher you rank in search results for the keywords that your content contains. But raising your authority score isn't as simple as editing your content.

Google uses many factors to create this rating, and although there are things we can do to influence it, there's no strict rules that make it easy. Some of the factors include things like how old your domain name is and what kind of internal linking structure you have.

But by far the biggest factor in determining your site's authority score is your backlinks. A backlink is when someone else's site links back to yours. For example, if you have a listing on your association website, that listing can often have a link back to your site. It will show your name and have your website address beneath it as a clickable link.

When Google looks around the internet it sees all the other sites that have links to yours, and each of those links is like a vote for your site. The more backlinks you have, and the more highly those sites themselves are ranked, the higher your authority score becomes. So getting more backlinks is one of the most important things you can do to help your site rank well in the organic search results.

However, backlinks are not under your direct control. You have to get in touch with the people running other sites and ask them to link to you, or be so awesome that people link to you by themselves without being asked. Either way, it's not necessarily quick or simple... but it works.

 ## USEFUL TOOL: OPEN SITE EXPLORER

https://moz.com/researchtools/ose/

Open Site Explorer is an online tool that shows an estimate of your page's authority score. This is useful as you make changes to your site and develop it over time, to see how your improvements are tracking. But more importantly, this tool also lists backlinks for any page you enter into it, and then also estimates how powerful each of those backlinks is.

This makes it a fantastic research tool and a way to source websites that may be open to linking to you. For example, search for larger or older competitor businesses, especially if they appear higher in search results than you. Using this tool you can see what other sites are linking to theirs – which means you can contact some of those sites too and see if they'll link to you as well.

You'll find that the free version of Open Site Explorer only lets you perform three website checks each day. That's okay – check what you can, then contact those backlink sites while you wait for the next day to do more searches.

GETTING HELP WITH SEO

Okay, we know what you're thinking right now. Wouldn't it be easier to hire someone else to do this for you? Google results can be powerful in attracting new clients, but getting it to work seems kind of technical and mysterious. (And we're only covering the basics here – imagine what the pros must look at.)

Like any other marketing activity, getting help with SEO can be a good path, but only if the results you see are worth the money you spend. And by results, we mean bookings.

Considering that SEO service packages would often start at $200 per month and rise quickly from there, you should see a good number of bookings each month to justify the investment. Look back at your client acquisition cost to see your goal.

There are some marketing companies in this industry that charge top dollar but do very little work, and they get away with it precisely because SEO seems "kind of technical and mysterious" and truly is a little unpredictable. So poor results can be blamed on "competition" or "algorithm changes". Plus, it often takes two or three months to see any impact SEO has on your Google results anyway, which makes it hard to see what is happening quickly.

So if you're choosing someone to help you, look at the tasks they will perform each month as part of your plan. A common monthly SEO service would suggest content changes to your website, plus create backlinks from other websites each month – often by having a writer create and post articles onto other blogs around the internet, on your behalf. Each article contains a link back to your site, so it helps with your site authority. Get the company you hire to send you links to the articles they write each month and anything else they create, so that they are accountable for the action tasks they have and not just the end result.

BLOGGING

Creating a blog on your website, where you write regular short articles, is very useful to build out the top of your funnel, for three reasons:

- Firstly, it is a powerful addition to your site's SEO and helps you get found in Google's search results. Google loves regular new content on a site, showing it is active and useful. Plus each blog post is essentially a new page on your site, with its own potential to have recognised keywords to appear under, and its own unique topic of interest.

- Blogging also gives you perfect content to share through social media. Each time you write a post, the topic should align with your content plan so that it adds to the mountain of value you provide to your clients. Then share your post on social media and email it to your clients so that it's seen by your tribe, reinforcing your authority on the topic and giving helpful advice or insight at the same time.

- Finally, blogging gives other websites a reason to link to you. If you have a helpful resource of articles, you'll find that other businesses will share them on their own social pages, and you may even find they mention you on their own websites or blogs.

The articles you write in your blog also show readers what topics you know and care about, and they give people helpful advice, education or entertainment. This makes them perfect middle-of-funnel content as people can spend time with them and get to know and trust you more.

How do I blog?

Always have your blog as part of your website so that it's easy to find for clients and you can maximise the Google search benefits. To create this part of your site, many of the popular website editors have a simple option to turn it on. For example, if you are using WordPress, the ability to blog is built into the system and simply needs to be enabled in your theme and given a menu link so that readers can find it. If you are having trouble, ask your website support team or a local web developer for help.

Once you have the tech sorted out, you should be able to add posts or articles with a simple text area, a main photo, and the ability to embed other photos or videos within the main text area of your article.

Aim for 300 to 400 words per article you write, and write at least once a month. If you can't commit to a minimum monthly schedule then it's better not to have the blog at all – it can actually give a negative perception if the most recent content is months old, and it leaves people wondering if your business is still active.

There are different styles of posts, so feel free to be creative. Select a topic that you know your audience will want to hear about. A good source of content is noticing what gets brought up in conversation by your clients in treatment, or social media posts that have received good attention.

Create a powerful headline when you write, as this is what people see in search results or social shares, and it has the largest impact on whether or not people will click through to read the rest of the article. Write in a way that has a powerful connection with your audience around the topic you've chosen. Be as specific and clear as you can.

Likewise choose the feature image carefully as this is the one that will appear when the article is shared on Facebook.

As you write the text, keep your sentences and paragraphs short, and break up large areas of text using bullet points, subheadings or images. The web is a visual place so the layout of the text on screen needs to look clear and simple to understand so that people will read it.

Also, have fun! Writing a blog is one of the ways you connect with your audience so it should feel like a conversation that gives easy pieces of advice and connects you with the people who read it.

Phew! Well done, you made it. Let's get back to standard English now and leave the techno-babble behind.

Ultimately, if you're not appearing well enough in Google you can pay someone to help you, or sign up for Google AdWords Express, the paid Google advertising service which will guarantee that you appear in the search results for a reasonable fee. And no matter which way you go, always keep track of your spend so that you can compare your client acquisition cost to other tactics you use to attract clients. Google is awesome, but it's only one tool you have in your growing belt of business tools.

PART III
AMAZING MECHANICS

CHAPTER 10

BUILDING STRONG FOUNDATIONS

Building the mechanics of your business is where everything comes together as the different parts are combined into one unique and beautiful picture. The treatments you do, your mindset and your marketing all work together to create a business that serves your clients and supports your lifestyle. The mechanics are the systems and structures that sit beneath the other activities, so that the business performs smoothly, consistently and predictably.

In essence, these are the many "cogs in the machine" that make the business run. They include software, frameworks, procedures and tasks to outsource. We've used hundreds of different tools and methods for making our businesses work smoothly, and we've seen hundreds more being used by other therapists. What we will look at here are the foundational mechanics that you must have in place to be able to continue your journey up the Health Leader Ladder and ensure you won't burn out with your new-found action mindset.

WHY DO I NEED STRONG MECHANICS?

Having strong mechanics in your business saves you time, reduces stress, makes your life easier and keeps everything organised. Without this, things become disorganised and overwhelming as you rely on your own memory and time to do tasks over and over again. Mechanics become more important as your business grows, and they have a vital role in solving the new challenges that will appear as you become more successful.

There are essentially two methods that you as a leader can use to handle challenges in your business, and each has a totally different energy. As well as "mechanics", we call the other method "dynamics". Dynamics refers to the personality and enthusiasm you put into your business every day.

At the beginning of your journey up the Health Leader Ladder a lot of "dynamic" energy is required. You'll be putting yourself out there, marketing a lot, treating clients, building relationships, being energetic and colourful. This dynamic energy is the "bang" energy that makes it super fun and exciting to start new projects and get things off the ground. Some people love dynamics and are naturally good at this style of activity.

However, dynamics can't solve a mechanics problems. For example, if your staff are not getting paid on time or their pays are incorrect, a motivational speech and a friendly smile will only win them over for so long. You need a better payment system to ensure pays happen accurately and on time.

And that's what we're talking about with mechanics. As your business grows to the Rising Star and Successful levels, you build these systems and structures in place to ensure everything continues to run smoothly. If you find yourself doing the same repetitive, low-value tasks again and again, see how you can systemise them to become quicker or move them off your plate entirely. Likewise, every time you face a challenge in your growing business, think about what you can put in place so that it doesn't happen again or is easier to solve next time.

The more mechanics you can put in place over time, the easier and more fun your business becomes as you can focus on the activities you really love. So let's have a look at some of the mechanics and operations in your business, and how you can streamline them or improve them.

REBOOKING YOUR CLIENTS

A client base that is engaged with you and booking regular treatments is the backbone of a successful and sustainable practice. We don't train massage therapists on how to do treatments or create their health outcomes – that's a circle of genius that we leave to you as a therapist to discover through training, experience and other professional development that you do. But when your rebooking rate is high it means your treatment outcomes cross over into business outcomes. They support each other. It goes without saying that you must be at least a competent therapist if your business is going to thrive – whether those outcomes are remedial, relaxation or in any other form. The promise you give your clients that you will meet their needs must be fulfilled.

Now don't get this wrong. We're not saying you need to be a super-body-work-ninja to run a successful clinic. Not true! If you're qualified, you have everything you need to start treating people. The type of conditions or people you treat may change and grow over time, but you can start right now with everything you've been trained to treat already. We take it as a given that you are making most of your clients happy and giving them the outcomes they expect.

The next step is just as important.

In order for your business to grow you need to be seeing each of your clients multiple times. This could be for a planned course of treatments or as ongoing regular maintenance. Either way, your business needs regular clients coming in so that you can have more stability in your bookings and cashflow. It's also fantastic for your clients: once you accept that massage helps people then you should see it as part of your role to help them even more by encouraging them to receive treatment more often.

So how do you easily get people to rebook, without coming across as a sleazy salesperson? There's an easy three-step technique that will create a 95% rebooking rate when used correctly. We originally created this to teach our staff, and we now teach it to hundreds of other therapists around the world and regularly get thanks and feedback about the difference the results make for therapists and their businesses.

Greeting the customer

The first step is to have excellent customer service.

Greet your client when you see them, at the door or in reception if you have one. Use their name, and smile right up to your eyes. Be authentically happy to see them.

Listen carefully when you are doing your assessment at the start of the treatment, especially if it's the first time you've seen this client. You can go through their history with them verbally rather than asking them to fill out a form – this helps to build rapport with them as well as making the process more accurate and controlled.

During the massage

Step two takes place while you are performing your treatment.

As you're working on them, ask a few leading questions about massage, like, "How often do you have a massage?", or, "Have you thought about having regular massage?" Questions like this help to seed the idea of massage being a regular activity.

Another great conversation at this point is if you can share a very quick story of another client (keep it anonymous of course) who was in a similar situation to the person on the table right now, and how this other client now comes in regularly and finds it very beneficial.

When the client is leaving

The third step in this technique happens at the desk, when your client is leaving. At this point you need to remember that you are the Health Leader in this relationship and your client is relying on you to recommend the best next steps for them. As well as stretches and water, one of the next steps should be for them to come in and see you again.

This can be as simple as these 10 words, spoken with confidence and authority: "I'd like to see you again in a week's time". Then hold the space by not speaking, so that they have time to weigh up their options before they say, "Of course". The client still has the power to say no if they want to, but the easiest path presented to them is your recommendation to see them again.

If you're not yet confident with rebooking, practise the words beforehand. Rebook your spouse, your friends, your dog, or basically anyone until the words flow out of your mouth smoothly. Confidence is key, and the more you do it the more successful at it you will become.

As you improve your rebooking skills you'll find your client base begins to see you more often and your bookings and cashflow naturally improve.

SETTING YOUR PRICES

Pricing is another issue that some therapists struggle with. We often hear the question, "What should I charge?" It can be tricky for new businesspeople to set their prices well because they've often never been on the "selling" end of a business before, and have always been a "buyer" in the past.

Especially if you have just been studying, money may not be in abundance, and students usually do hundreds of hours of free massage as they are learning, so it's natural to set a very low price simply because that's what is around you as you begin. Or maybe you have a couple of clients who are struggling for money – like really struggling – and so you base your entire pricing strategy around those two people.

But setting a price that is too low doesn't do anyone any favours. Your business needs money to survive (and so do you), so if you want to be able to treat your clients well and build a long-term career in massage you must charge enough to keep your business healthy.

We often start our massage career as a consumer so continue to make decisions as one. But when we step into working for ourselves, we need to shift our thinking to *what does the business need?*

Here's the thing: as awesome as we all know that massage is, no-one is going to take food off their table to come and see you. The people who regularly get massage will usually have a car (or two), health insurance, plenty of food in their fridge and go out for dinner occasionally. In other words, they have discretionary money that they can choose to spend on what they want to.

And yet, some therapists will work for such a small pay rate that they themselves can't afford to pay their bills because "I couldn't possibly charge more in my socioeconomic area"... a story we hear weekly when speaking to therapists. These therapists are essentially taking food off their own table to support their clients who often don't need it.

The basis of business is supplying someone a service or product in return for money. It's a two-way relationship that works naturally and easily when it is balanced. So you support your clients in their health through your treatments and leadership. And let them support you financially in return.

Let us give you an example. We have two kids and they eat – *a lot!* So each week we do the shopping, and we have never had a checkout person apologise that our peas cost more this week than last week. Why? Because it's not their responsibility as to whether or not we can afford to do a $30 shop or a $300 shop. They simply offer their products and services and it's our responsibility as consumers to ensure we can pay for our groceries.

Just as it is your clients' choice to see you.

Why increasing your pricing can attract more clients

The typical price for massage anywhere across Australia is between $75 and $110 for a typical one-hour treatment, and $90 is an average and what we would recommend for most people. Obviously there are outliers above and below that range, and often these people feel very passionate about defending their price point and their reasons why.

Often the level of comfort a therapist has around charging what they're worth comes down to the life experiences they've had in the past. Someone who has worked on a cruise ship or at a high-end day spa where they charge $250 for a one-hour massage won't come back and charge $60 for a massage, no matter where they are based. Instead they'll usually charge $100-plus, and because they're totally fine with that their clients are too.

In fact, what we can tell you after speaking with hundreds of therapists is that those who charge $100 or more are almost never struggling for clients. They might have other challenges they need help with, however scarcity is not one of them. Partly this is because at that price point they have more cashflow to spend on marketing and advertising, so the circle of business perpetuates itself.

But we'd like you to look at it another way too.

For a normal buyer, pricing is often the single biggest indicator of quality. This means we naturally think that things that are more expensive are better quality. You can probably remember doing this yourself, for example when looking at buying a television or similar. If you're not a tech-head, many of the TVs look the same. Yet even ones that are the same size can vary widely in price. Why? It's simple to assume that there's something better about the more expensive TVs that we just don't know about until we see it in action.

It's the same with massage. As a practitioner you know what the different modalities mean, what value you have to offer, how you compare to other people in the area. But a normal person won't know that and will often look at price as a very simple way to tell who is "better".

The words we use to describe this are "reassuringly expensive".

It doesn't mean everyone will go to the most expensive person in town (not everyone wants to pay for quality even if they perceive that you're better), but there are plenty of people who will want to go to the "best" massage therapist and will use price to judge that before they come in.

So contrary to what your natural instincts might tell you, being cheaper usually isn't the best way to get more clients. Weird, right? If you're too cheap, people won't come at all. The more you charge (within the range of normal) the busier you get.

How do I raise my prices?

If you have decided to raise your prices after reading that last section, good on you. Here's how it's done:

- First of all, do not apologise. Price rises are normal, and if you treat them as a normal part of business, your clients will too.

- Once you make the decision, don't put it off. Don't wait until January or the new financial year or any other arbitrary time. You don't need the excuse of a specific date to make this change, just make the decision and start as soon as you can.

- Don't promote your price rise to the general public. If someone hasn't been in to see you before then they don't know your prices anyway, so there's no reason to tell them and it draws attention to the wrong part of your message. Only your existing clients need to know.

Once you decide on the new pricing, the first step is to update your signage in the clinic and prices on your website and in your booking software.

Then, the next day you start informing clients when you see them. You don't have to actually charge them the new amount on their first visit after the new pricing is set, but you let them know the change has already happened. For example, you could say to a regular client at the end of their session, "Hey, just letting you know that we had a price rise last week, so I'll charge you the old price today and next time you come in it will be $XX." Super friendly, super easy.

It's much easier to talk about a change that has already happened, because you don't need to defend it or excuse it. The decision has already been made and now you're doing them a small favour by giving them this current treatment at the old price. And here's the thing: 99% of people will say okay and not bat an eyelid. They're used to price rises happening on everything they buy.

But know this too – you will have two people who complain. Just expect it! They are not the average sum of all your other clients and they shouldn't prevent you from making the changes you need to. Now that you know, you can say to yourself that they are just the two people you have been warned about, and keep on going with your business.

If you're not charging enough right now, make the change tomorrow – *you've got this!*

CHAMPION SNAPSHOT: KHLOE SYLLEBRANQUE

Khloe had moved to Australia only a couple of years before we met her. When we first spoke she was charging only $65 per treatment and only had a handful of clients each month. She was nervous about raising her prices, so when she did she promoted relaxation massage at $75 and remedial at $90. To her surprise (and delight) hardly anyone ever booked the lower-price treatment, so she soon stopped offering it altogether. Khloe also found a new confidence in herself and proactively promoted herself as a niche specialist. Within six months she became fully booked at full price and continued to grow demand, so she introduced a membership model so clients could book their regular treatments for months ahead. It's now a year since she started and she needs a new premises to keep up with demand!

UNDERSTANDING YOUR FINANCES

Once you're charging an amount to create a sustainable income, it's important that you know a few basic things about finances and money and how this side of business works.

Some people understand their figures so well that they are on the pulse of their business all the time and know what money will be in their bank account before they even look. These people understand how many treatments they need to do, what payments will come out of their account, and how to balance this all out so that they can take home the regular amount they want to pay themselves each week.

Other people find it all a bit confusing, and they end up taking money out of their business account when they need to pay bills but they never really know if they're getting ahead or behind or what expenses are coming up that they need to plan for. Businesses can limp along like this, but if you want to build a strong business you must understand your numbers.

If you've already been running your business for a while or have a good head for figures you probably belong to the first category already, and if that's you, feel free to skim through this part. But, if you don't yet understand your numbers or find it overwhelming sometimes, this is vitally important – so tune in.

The basics

Let's start with a really simple look at four important financial basics: turnover, expenses, profit and breakeven.

The "turnover" of your business is all the money that comes into your bank account. If you charge $90 and you see 20 clients in a week, you have turned over $1800.

As you would already know, running a business has "expenses". You'll spend money on things like oil, marketing, washing,

"For, in the end, it is impossible to have a great life unless it is a meaningful life. And it is very difficult to have a meaningful life without meaningful work."

Jim Collins

insurance, rent, association fees, business coaching, professional development and anything else you purchase for the business.

The money from your turnover that is left over after these expenses is your "profit". Often this is what you then pay yourself as the business owner.

So if your turnover is $1800 and your expenses are $750, then you have made a profit of $1050 for the week. You should set aside 30% of this for tax ($315), and another 9.5% for superannuation (rounded to $100). Together these add up to $415 in this example.

Put this amount into a separate account until it's needed, either a high-interest savings account or mortgage offset account. We also recommend estimating on the high side so that you are putting away more than is eventually needed; the extra will build up into a bit of a war chest for when times might get more difficult.

Then you pay yourself the remaining $635, or whatever part of that you choose.

The term "breakeven" refers to another really important number for you to know: the minimum number of treatments you must do each week to cover all your expenses.

In the example above, if your weekly expenses are $750 and you charge $85 per treatment you can work out that you'll need to do nine treatments in a week, which would bring in $765, slightly better than breakeven. Treatments above nine is where you begin to bring in profit. (There are some per-treatment expenses like laundry and oils, but we're keeping it really simple in this example so you get the main idea.)

Also hear this: as your business grows, a bookkeeper is your best friend. In fact, the very first thing we recommend outsourcing is bookkeeping. A reliable and trustworthy bookkeeper takes care of the numbers for you, can often submit your BAS for you, and prepares everything for your accountant to review.

GST

In Australia, you are required to register and charge 10% GST (Goods and Services Tax) as soon as your business turns over $75,000 or more.

What this means is that you must charge GST on top of your fees and pay this to the government. You will need to collect it on all items that you sell. You will be required to record this by submitting a BAS (Business Activity Statement) quarterly through a registered BAS agent (or you can do it yourself).

When you're registered you will also get a refund of any GST you have paid to other businesses over the quarter, which means you are only required to pay the difference. This part of it is kind of nice, but for any business that's running well you'll always generate more income than expenses so you'll always have to pay more GST than you claim back. If you consistently get a GST refund on your BAS it can be a sign that your business is in trouble.

Reaching the GST turnover point can feel a bit painful, as it requires you to action a 10% price rise but none of that 10% goes to you; it's tax that is paid directly to the government. So you have the hassle of a price rise without the benefits of more money in your pocket.

COLLECTING AND ANALYSING CRITICAL DATA

As your business grows your focus on numbers will expand way beyond just looking at the dollars.

In our office we have a sign that reads, "What gets measured, gets done".

As a business owner you need to know certain numbers that give clarity on how your business is tracking. When you know the numbers to look at they become like a dashboard for your business, giving you feedback and insight that help you drive better.

There are specific things that we recommend you track each week that are the perfect dashboard numbers for a massage business. Watching these numbers brings stability to the business and confidence to you as you know what happens each week. Without a dashboard to guide you, you may be guilty of judging your business based on how you feel in the moment, rather than facts. For example, if you have a busy week you will feel very excited and happy. Or if you have a quiet week or a bunch of cancellations, you will feel down and start having thoughts that your business is going nowhere. But none of this is based on data.

Rather than taking this short-term path based on momentary emotions, if you have some numbers to analyse it will help you know and understand where you really are and also see what you can tweak. We call these important dashboard numbers your "critical data".

Let's have a look at some of the critical data numbers you can track:

- number of massages you had booked at the start of the week

- number of massages you actually performed – to compare with the above

- your rebooking rate – as a percentage

- your average transaction spend

- total turnover for the week

- how many new clients you saw

- how many online bookings came through

- how many Facebook ads you do
- did you send an email newsletter?
- did you write any blogs?
- any other meaningful marketing activities.

Track these in a simple spreadsheet every week and you'll soon see the patterns. For example, you might start to see that you always have 10 people booked in at the start of the week but end up with five new bookings on average, for a total of 15. So don't sweat it at the start of the week as you know what will happen.

If your rebooking rate is low it will be very hard to build up a consistent client base, so keeping an eye on that is very important. If you're not investing in marketing you won't attract as many new clients. If you need to increase your average dollar spend, look for some products to sell or offer longer or upgraded treatments.

The more history and data you collect the more you will learn. After a year or two you'll see what months are busier and what months are quieter. This brings some certainty to your business and allows you to see your business success coming from the numbers rather than how you feel in the moment.

QUICK CASH PACKAGES

There will be times in the business when you need to increase the flow of money in the short term with a large "lump" of income. This might be before taking time off or when your BAS is due, or if you want to expand. Whatever the reason, having a way to create quick cash can be a lifesaver in times of need.

A great way of doing this is to create a special package deal that is available only to a select few existing clients. The great thing about a package is that you get paid a single lump sum up front.

The bonus for the buyer is that they get a discount or special offer in return.

It's important to see this as a special offer or event – one of the very few where we ever recommend discounting – and for that reason it's offered privately to selected clients only and should never be promoted publically.

The purpose of this strategy is quick cashflow, so you want the package to be high value, ideally $600 to $1000. To create an appealing package, you can bundle treatments together and include products that you might sell, upgrade the first massage to 90 minutes, or get creative with your bonuses. Then promote the package to a handful of your VIP clients, and keep it exclusive by only ever having a limited number available; for example, five only. Exclusive packages and offers can be exciting for the clients who receive them, as they feel good just by being given the offer, whether or not they take it up. So when you have identified who you'll make the offer to, talk it up to them: send out an email or send a letter to a few of them, then give them a call or talk about it when they come in next.

You can also have special packages available for groups in your community. These may be completely public or may be available only to members of the groups you work with, but either way these packages are treated more as a marketing avenue. You can discount if you want to make it more attractive, but not as heavily – try to think of other bonuses to include instead. For example, we had a "personal trainer" package that we would use with PTs in our local community, that they could offer their members. For us the packages included either four 60-minute massages or four 30-minute massages. We upgraded their first massage for an extra 30 minutes and added in some products that would help muscle recovery and exercise.

The advantage to this is tripled, because the trainer is able to offer something special to their clients that makes them look good, the client gets a great deal on a package that will help them reach their goals, and you gain a new client in the process. This is why partner programs like this are so ideal, because everybody wins.

One of the problems with these strategies is that if you sell too many packages at a discount you have to continue to honour the treatments down the track. This bites into cashflow in the future, so ensure you don't overuse this approach to the point of shooting yourself in the foot. Use with caution!

Making money is one of the most important aspects to a business, but you can't have what you don't value yourself. If you struggle with your attitude or habits around money personally, this will overflow into how you interact with your clients and you'll find the patterns keep repeating. If this is you, spend some time working on your beliefs and mindset around money. Be authentic and whole-hearted in your approach, and see how you can make your finances align with and support the heart-centred goals you have for your business. We call this "heart-centred success".

Money is the lifeblood of your business. With money flowing, you can treat more clients, grow your influence and build a long-term career. Without it, nothing can happen and the business will fail. The more you work on it the better your business will be.

CHAPTER 11

MAKING EVERYTHING YOU DO EASIER

Along with money, the second most important resource for business success is time – your time, as the business developer and owner. What you spend your time on has a direct impact on what happens in your business. A business that is starved of time or attention becomes stagnant and dies, whereas a business with a proactive owner who spends time on learning and business development grows and flourishes.

SYSTEMS ARE SEXY

At the start, it's actually easier to balance your time. It doesn't always feel like it because there's so much to do! But at the start of a business you often work by yourself and don't have so many bookings, so it's easier to manage everything just by keeping it in your head or using a simple diary. You can get away with doing things manually at the start.

But as your business grows and you move up the Health Leader Ladder, you'll be busier with clients and other business activities and you'll find your time eaten up by the manual way of doing things. At this point you need to find ways to leverage your time better so that you can use it in more resourceful ways and get more outcomes from the energy you're putting in, so you need to start seeing systems as sexy rather than boring.

This is even more important when you hire staff. You want to be in a position where every staff member you hire makes your life easier, but if you have poor systems you will find it's the opposite: each team member you hire will take more of your time.

Procedure manuals

The first structured system we're going to look at here is a very simple way of making your life easier, by creating a procedure manual. A procedure manual is a set of written instructions showing how to do all the common tasks you do in your business. It's like an instruction manual.

It's useful for you to use yourself, because it makes it easier to remember exactly how to do things that you might not do every day. It's also a fabulous way of getting your staff to help with business tasks while still keeping everything consistent to the standard you set. If you don't have staff yet, create a procedure manual anyway so that when you do hire, it's already there. Even if you just have a partner or other person help out occasionally, having procedures to follow keeps everything neat.

Create a system or procedure for everything you do on a regular basis in your business. The level of detail you'll need depends on the size of your team or your potential team. If it's just you, you will do well to create some systems for yourself which might allow you to outsource, or to be ready for when you do add staff.

If you have a team of three to five people, your systems become even more important, and if you have a team of 20 your systems will be more detailed and complex and will be essential for the business to run smoothly. You can't have 20 people all doing things their own way. There are two areas that must be systematised first: admin and your massage procedures.

Admin

This includes all the things that happen around the outside of the treatments you perform:

- how to make a booking

- how to change a booking

- how to take a payment

- how to make a rebooking (what you say or your script, as well as how to make that booking in your system)

- how to sell a gift voucher

- how to settle your HICAPS machine

- how you store the receipts

- how you record your notes.

Your perfect massage every time

This is a run-through of your client treatment and management process, which includes:

- how you greet a client

- what you say when they arrive

- how you take them through to the treatment room

- how you take their history

- how you drape your clients
- how you finish the treatment
- how you leave the room
- how you then greet them when they come out of the room.

You may think that all this seems a little silly right now and that even when you bring on board team members surely they will just know how to do all this. The problem is that everyone is different and will have different ideas and ways of doing things. Even another great therapist will do things differently to you, and your clients will be used to your way and standard of doing things. Systemising keeps consistency in your treatments and your business as you grow.

PLANNING YOUR SYSTEM CREATION – IT'S EASIER THAN YOU THINK

Creating your entire procedure manual can be a big job, but luckily it doesn't have to be done all at once. Systemisation is a process. Most of the time people overestimate what they need to do in this area – once it's begun, you can tailor it to your needs and simply write procedures for each item.

To get started, plan out everything you will need to systemise and put a date next to it that you will have it done by. People often think that they have to systemise everything *today* and become overwhelmed. But that doesn't help! The most important thing to do is to get moving on it. All you need to do is set aside about an hour a week to make a start. Wherever you are at the moment, pick a couple of the most important things you do and write simple instructions of how to do them.

"I've learned that people will forget what you said, people will forget what you did, but people will never forget how you made them feel."

Maya Angelou

Once you have the first few systems nailed down, break down a list of the next most important and create one a week until you're done. You can write your procedure in a simple Word or Google doc, or use something more sophisticated like an online private portal with a login for your staff.

CHAMPIONS SNAPSHOT: CHLOË PARSONSON

Chloë had been in business for three years when we first met. She had a reasonable number of regular clients but no systems in place to manage them, and knew she needed to have minor surgery, which would require three weeks off.

Chloë is incredibly dedicated, so one of the first things she did was get the right team member on board and then write up the most vital procedures in the business, so that the new therapist could replicate everything Chloë did. This allowed Chloë to rest and recover with minimum interruptions.

As it turns out the team member left a little while later, but Chloë has gone on to double her business turnover while restricting her own hours to five days per weeks, and has just booked an overseas holiday to celebrate her progress.

Online options can also allow for different styles of learning, using pictures or video as well as written instructions. Some people need to hear you say what you need, others like to see it, some need to feel it, and some need checklists. In an online portal you can create checklists and then record a video showing how to work through it. Like if you're a towel pedant like Elicia was; she always wanted the towels rolled in a specific way. This came from her day spa days of rolling 300 towels each week and then having to look at them on the shelf when they were doing massages all day. The towel edge needed be at the back of the shelf and the fold to the front, and it also needed to be rolled firmly so that they could be stacked and not just folded around. This is difficult to describe but can be demonstrated in a video.

Whatever your particular quirks and preferences, you can create a quick video on your phone and upload that to your portal. This allows the staff access to see how you do things with a demonstration as well as the written instructions.

BOOKING SOFTWARE AND ONLINE BOOKINGS

Booking software is an amazing time saver and convenience as it allows your clients to book online after visiting your website or Facebook page. This is a massive boost to your online marketing because so many people who find you on Google or see your Facebook ads will want to take the next step of booking in right then and there. Online bookings makes this easy.

Most booking software includes options to allow new clients to do online bookings or just regulars. It's always better to have it open for everyone so that you can encourage those easy new bookings, but if you work from home or are nervous about safety you can restrict it to existing clients only, so that you can screen new clients by phone before accepting them.

However, be aware that booking software alone will not attract new clients. What it will do is get new clients on board more easily. The right software will also connect a bunch of other things for you in your business and allow you to track some of that amazing critical data more easily (see chapter 10). The right booking software can help you track your finances for tax purposes, manage compliance for health funds, send SMS reminders for client appointments, and perform other marketing functions. You can also manage your calendar online from wherever you are.

By the time you are seeing 5 to 10 clients a week, you need to get booking software. There are many options on the market, which range from free to $250 a month depending on your needs. When it comes time to choose, look for advice from other therapists about what is popular right now: people are always willing to share why they love the one they chose or why they hated the last one they had. Ask in the Massage Business Support Network on Facebook and you'll get great responses to help you choose.

Ultimately, you need to decide between the various options by looking at your current needs and your future growth. The things we think are important are:

- ability for clients to do online bookings (vital)

- integration with your bookkeeping software

- SMS and email reminders

- online payments for pre-paying and gift vouchers (although this can be done externally to the software)

- clinical note taking

- option to scan and upload a PDF attachment of your client's history form

- option to enter how people heard about you

- you can export your data if you choose to change applications down the track.

Most of the services will offer a free trial, so try a few out and see which one is going to work for you and your business.

MEETING YOUR COMPLIANCE OBLIGATIONS

In Australia, massage is an unregulated (or self-regulated) industry. We are governed by our associations and their codes of conduct, rather than any specific government guidelines, and membership of an association is optional. What this means is that essentially anyone can call themselves a massage therapist, and even if they are not qualified in the way an association expects, they can simply choose not to join one and carry on. The thing is, they're usually uninsured so it's a risky way to run a business, and they're also opting out of the mainstream industry and the support it provides.

Massage associations

You need to be a member of a recognised association to get your health fund provider numbers. This makes it easier for your clients to claim rebates from private health funds. For example, you have the option to use HICAPS, which is an EFTPOS machine that will allow your clients to swipe their health fund card and receive a rebate on the spot.

Membership also makes it easier and cheaper to get public liability and professional indemnity insurance, which are a must for anyone in business of any kind. Plus, being an association member shows you are working to a recognised professional standard and take your career seriously. The good associations also provide opportunity for ongoing professional development and other important help for therapists.

So, being a member of one of the professional associations is essential as far as we are concerned. There are a few to choose from, the largest in Australia being Massage & Myotherapy Australia (MMA) and Australian Massage Therapy Association (AMTA). Look at these two and others, and ask for recommendations from other therapists to see what benefits they find from each and what else is available.

To join and maintain your association membership you must follow certain rules and regulations, which is fair enough – the role of the association is maintaining the professionalism of the industry and representing their clients to health funds and government. Following the rules of your association is what we call "compliance". Each of them will have specific items, but they'll always include things like you must maintain a current first aid certificate and continue participating in professional education.

Health funds

Besides association rules, it's also important to know what other areas you may need to be compliant in. For example, something to be very clear on here is that if you offer health fund rebates you enter into an agreement individually with every health fund that you offer rebates for. Some funds will require certain things on their invoices, some will have requirements on how your files are stored, and some will have protocols for you to follow with new clients.

And always remember, your provider number is *your* provider number. We have all heard of places that will have one provider number for a bunch of unqualified therapists and they all use that one number to claim. You must never do this. You must not do this for another team member, even if they are qualified and maybe fell off the list because they didn't submit their insurance. You also must not allow your clients to have treatments on behalf of their children and claim those when their benefits run out.

Health funds take their rules very seriously, so you must read through all of the agreements. If you are ever audited, you will be held to these standards. Take the time out to read them and know how important they are.

The National Code of Conduct and your obligations

The Health Complaints Commissioner (HCC) has the National Code of Conduct for General Health Services, which covers any health service that does not come under AHPRA (basically all massage and myotherapy and most other complementary health services). This was finalised on 1 February 2017, when Tasmania came on board to unify this and make it national.

This gives our clients somewhere to go to make a complaint if they feel the need to. What it means for us as practitioners is that we must adhere to the code. This list is some of the highlights, but read the full thing for more information. We must display the code where we practise, like our qualifications, and:

- provide safe and ethical healthcare

- obtain consent for treatment

- take care to protect clients from infection

- minimise harm and act appropriately if something goes wrong

- report concerns about other practitioners

- keep appropriate records and comply with privacy laws

- be covered by insurance

- display information about the code of conduct and making a complaint.

We must *not*:

- mislead clients about our products, services or qualifications

- put clients at risk due to our own physical or mental health problems

- practise under the influence of drugs or alcohol

- make false claims about curing serious illnesses, such as cancer
- exploit clients financially
- have an inappropriate relationship with a client
- discourage clients from seeking other healthcare or refuse to cooperate with other practitioners if they do.

If any of these requirements have been breached, the client can contact the HCC and an investigation can begin.

 DOWNLOAD: CODE OF CONDUCT

To read the complete Code of Conduct and display it in your workspace you can download it in poster format it on the HCC website at:

https://hcc.vic.gov.au/sites/default/files/code_of_conduct_full_text_a3_poster.pdf

Other requirements

There are also other requirements you must follow as a healthcare provider. The two biggest reasons therapists get into trouble are not draping effectively and not writing client notes.

Firstly, as Elicia used to teach her students when she taught the ethics unit in the Diploma of Remedial Massage, use the biggest bath sheets you can find. This makes it easier to drape and helps give confidence to your clients. Always get consent to treat and only expose the areas you need to work on.

When it comes to writing treatment notes, they form part of a legal document. They can be used in court to prove an existing condition, show what was treated in a session, or even as an alibi for your client. Preferably, your notes should have your testing pre and post, details of the treatment itself, and any follow-up required. These notes should be written on the day of treatment or within 24 hours, and you must include the date you wrote them.

If you are audited by a health fund and you do not have adequate documentation, you will be required to pay back any rebates that you do not have documentation for as well as possible fines, and you may face more stringent auditing for a prolonged period of time.

So write your notes. Yes, it's boring. Yes, you're going to be tired at the end of the day. Booking software usually has a note-taking feature, which will save you a bunch of time. You can also set up your own formula that works for you. Whatever way you do it, write your notes. *Write your notes.*

YOU'RE NOW A MECHANICAL GENIUS

Phew! You made it.

In this part we've examined the most important mechanics in the back end of your business, and once you have them in place your business is ready for the next level of growth.

Mechanics might not seem "sexy", and you can easily make the mistake of thinking that you should wait until your business is really busy before you tackle them, but to be successful these are just as important to master as your massage skills. And just like your massage skills, you might not rock at all the mechanics right from the start. But when you commit to learning and creating, you'll gain experience as you walk your business journey, and that experience makes everything flow more easily.

PART IV

NEXT STEPS FOR GROWTH

CHAPTER 12

THE FOUR PILLARS FOR GROWING YOUR BUSINESS

We saw at the start of this book that a six-figure business can be achieved through consistently performing 25 treatments each week yourself and charging a reasonable amount for them. However, getting to the six-figure mark with this method is only possible when you are fully booked (or very close to), and then it's almost impossible to increase beyond that amount. There's a natural ceiling created by the number of treatments that can physically be performed by an individual. And the amount of work this requires you to do is physically taxing on your body and simply not possible for therapists who have other time commitments. So a better way to increase your income is to take the next steps of growth by leveraging your time in better ways.

What do we mean by "leveraging" your time?

Well, the normal way a therapist gets paid is by getting paid by one person for one treatment, often per hour. To leverage your time more, you need to find ways to get paid by multiple people at once for the same amount of time. When done well this boosts you out of the direct "time for money" exchange and gives you far more earning potential. This is where you are climbing up the Health Leader Ladder beyond the first three rungs, and you're at the Rising Star stage moving into or though Successful.

THE FOUR GROWTH PILLARS

There are basically four ways that you can leverage your time better as a massage therapist and Health Leader. We call these the four "Growth Pillars" because they help hold your business up and make it stronger:

Growth Pillar 1: Scale with staff – a team can perform more treatments than you can alone.

Growth Pillar 2: Run workshops – get multiple people in a room.

Growth Pillar 3: Sell products – including network marketing.

Growth Pillar 4: Create an online program – which can be an upsell or bonus to your existing clients, or something to attract new people in.

Exactly what your next step looks like will depend on your natural talents, training and preferences, the opportunities in your area, and what sort of clients you work with.

When you're ready for this level, brainstorm your ideal business and map out which pillars it will include. Then start building it one pillar at a time – that way things are completed more quickly and you can begin to see the benefits of your actions sooner, without having to wait for all the work on every pillar to be complete.

It's like if you've ever seen a performer spinning plates. Getting each plate up there requires focus and energy, as the spinning starts and the balance is set up. But once they are up, each plate only needs tweaking in order to stay spinning beautifully, and that's when the performer moves onto putting the next plate up. Imagine if she tried to put 12 plates in the air at the same time? Impossible. But by doing them one at a time she makes it look effortless.

In this part of the book we will introduce each of these pillars to show you what the next steps will look like, and how to create this level of leverage when you're ready for it.

It's important to realise the place of these Growth Pillars in your business. Some of them will help you become fully booked in your solo practice, because they will build your reputation and become a cross-sell and upsell opportunity to new and existing clients. But the primary purpose of them is not necessarily to grow clients, it's to grow your business. Remember the ladder concept – build your foundations first and then create these pillars as you move up a rung or two.

We will give you the information you need to get started and see which ones appeal to you, and then when you begin to implement them you'll be able to see what areas you need more clarity around.

The same mindset and marketing skills you've built to improve your solo therapy business and climb the first few rungs of the ladder will also help you take these next steps. However, there will be a bunch of new skills you'll need to learn as well, and maybe even some rules that you'll need to "unlearn" as things change in your business.

What we love most about these pillars is that every single one of them builds your business while producing better health outcomes for your clients. All of them allow you to impact your clients more often and in new ways. And the best thing about this is that you've already got a huge head start on people who are trying to create these opportunities from scratch. Because you are already in business, you already have clients and you know what they need and what you can do for them.

You're already leading your tribe into better health.

 ## EXERCISE: VISUALISE YOUR FUTURE

If you could choose any of these four pillars to grow your business, whether that's right now or in the future, which ones would you choose? You have your own unique talents and tribe. What will serve them the best?

CHAPTER 13

GROWTH PILLAR 1: SCALE WITH STAFF

Scaling your business by hiring a team often seems like the most natural way for a therapist to grow their business, so this is a very popular pillar for people as they progress. It can seem like it will be easy because all you need to do is more of what you're already doing – you can grow organically by getting other therapists on board and growing your client base in the same ways you have been already. *Right?*

This is somewhat true. *Somewhat.*

In some ways it is straightforward to replicate yourself, and it certainly scales your time. You may spend only three or four hours each week managing a small team that can do three or four times the number of treatments you could perform just on your own. It can also be really fun and rewarding to mentor newer therapists as they gain experience and maturity in the industry, and it's fun and fulfilling to be part of a team that is enthusiastically and joyfully working towards a common goal.

Let's look at some of the issues you need to be aware of if you decide to build a team.

HOW TO HIRE LEGALLY

In the massage and health industries there are three common ways to engage additional people:

- employ (casual, part time or full time)
- use independent contractors
- rent a room out.

In the past the most common form of engagement has been the independent contractor model (sometimes called subcontracting). An example of this would be where a business owner pays a contractor a percentage of fees to come in and treat clients.

Unfortunately, most of these traditional contractor agreements are not seen as legally legitimate since the *Fair Work Act 2009* came in. The government has created a list of things they check in each situation to define if a worker is legitimately independent or if they are an employee... and the bad news is that many of the things they check make them see most independent contracts as "sham" contracts and deem that the workers are actually employees.

The vital thing to understand here is that it's *not a choice*. Even if you and your staff agree on the terms of a contract (or use a verbal agreement or handshake), the ATO or Fair Work can still do a random audit and find you in breach of the rules – whether you know the rules or not! If you're found to be in breach you can face fines of over $10,000 per staff member and be forced to back pay any entitlements the government deems you should have been paying, like holiday pay and superannuation. And it's you as the business owner that bears all the risk here – the worker will not be fined if a mistake is made (in fact, they'll likely end up with some extra back pay as a bonus).

For this reason we recommend staying well clear of independent contracts unless you have a special situation and an HR specialist has given you the okay to use them.

Instead, employ the staff you wish to have on board. It's easier than you think, and it gives both you and your staff rights and responsibilities that are well balanced. Casual employment means that if there are no bookings for a shift the staff member simply doesn't come to work and isn't paid, so this can be a good way to start with new staff so that they understand their responsibilities for rebooking and providing amazing service. Once they are established, moving to part time can give them and you a little more certainty around hours and roles.

 USEFUL TOOL: ATO EMPLOYER OR CONTRACTOR?

The ATO provides a simple quiz tool you can fill out to get an idea of whether they would see your staff as employees or contractors. Use the tool online here:

**https://www.ato.gov.au/Calculators-and-tools/
Employee-or-contractor/**

The other way to get more people on board is to let them truly run their own business and you simply rent space to them. This means you would charge a fixed day or half-day rate (or per week if they are busy enough) regardless of how many clients they see. In this case they would have their own business name and keep their own client records as well – you're essentially a landlord – but if there are multiple businesses doing this from the one space it can still feel like a team. You can encourage everyone to share marketing, to learn from each other and to cross-refer clients.

TEAM CHALLENGES

Scaling with staff in any way is also more challenging personally than you might realise. Leading and managing a team of other people requires skills that are very different from those you have as a solo therapist.

One of the biggest mistakes therapists make in their first hire is to assume that everyone will be the same as them – in treatment style, values and work ethic. They might look for a "diploma with a pulse", give them minimal training beyond showing them a few ropes… and then expect that new therapist to operate like them, at the same level, immediately.

We can tell you from years of our own experience and through working with hundreds of clients… this mistake is the quickest way to create massive frustrations in your business, set you on the burnout train and make your business fail. And the worst thing is that many therapists who make this mistake on their first hire never go back to learn how to do it better, so they remain stuck where they are.

You do need to document everything that happens on a consistent basis in your business and it is not the exciting side of business, however it will ensure that as you scale your business and bring on board team members you will achieve the same amazing results and keep frustrations to a minimum.

So, now that the hard news is out of the way, how should you bring on board staff in your business? It starts with this one principle, which is by far the most important: create an amazing environment.

You need to create the culture in your business that you love, a culture that's a reflection of you, and one where your values are lived and breathed through the fabric of the business, day in, day out. What it means when this is done right is that you *love* coming work every day, frustrations are minimal, and everyone around you is thriving.

WHAT IS THE "ENVIRONMENT"?

The "environment" is the intangible stuff that you can't see. The culture, the feel, the unwritten social codes that control how you and your team interact with each other and clients.

An awesome environment supports everyone at your workplace to be empowered, unified, productive, and to have fun doing it. A poor environment is the opposite. There's tension in the air, and everyone just wants to get out of there at the end of the day.

It comes down to the expectations that are inferred but not explicitly written down. Like, for example, you wouldn't wear bikinis to church, right? Why not? Because it's the wrong environment. But you might wear them to the beach, because that is the right environment.

Imagine going into a café that you just don't feel welcome in, and you're not really sure why. Then you go into a different café and it's just happening, it has a great vibe, you feel welcome and it's nice. There is a café in our hometown that we both love, called Driftwood. There are over a dozen other cafés in that small shopping centre as well, but Driftwood is the best (and the busiest). Firstly, their coffee is amazing! But more than that, their staff are always friendly and they source great local produce. They use reclaimed timber in all their interior fit-out. They take part in local events and fundraise for the local primary schools. Ultimately, when you walk into the café it feels great… and it's hard to tell exactly why. It's intangible. This café has created an amazing environment, and they are seeing the rewards: loyal clients, long-term staff and a successful business.

So how can you create a powerful environment like this for your business?

Creating a staff niche

So just like you have a niche or avatar for attracting clients you love working on, when you are hiring you need to create a niche or avatar for attracting the right staff.

Be super clear on who you want and what kind of behaviour you love. This starts by understanding your big picture mission, vision and values, so that you are hiring what we call a "values match". This is someone who almost gets what you do before they even start working for you, and loves doing things the way you love doing them.

CHAMPION SNAPSHOT: NICOLA SMITH

Nicola ran a massage and wellness centre that was working okay but she had to work a lot of hands-on hours herself to keep it going. By focusing on the environment of the business and creating great systems she was able to release some of her time, and then by becoming super clear on her staff niche she has grown to a team of eight that fits together beautifully. All because Nicola had massive clarity about what she wanted her business to look like and who she wanted to work with, and then she took the action to set her business up in the way to make it happen.

This comes from being super clear on your mission. At one point in our clinic we had hired a bunch of therapists and we were learning who was great and who wasn't a fit. Elicia was also teaching part of the Diploma of Remedial Massage at TAFE and she had a young man in her class who was always engaged in the conversation, handed work in on time, and was a friendly and personable student. He and Elicia just "clicked". Elicia watched the way he conducted himself, then had an "aha" moment and realised this was how clear she needed to be with the kind of staff she wanted.

She hired him, and he was great. (Hot tip: get them young in their career and train them!)

HOW TO HIRE SUPERSTAR THERAPISTS AND RECEPTION STAFF

Finding a new staff member can take time, especially when you want to make sure you're finding the exact right person.

And finding them is only the first step. Training them and then guiding them through their first few weeks is just as important, to ensure they are up to speed quickly and can connect with your way of doing things. We call this "onboarding", and without it your new staff will feel lost and alone. And some aspects of employment are regulated by government and require the paperwork that goes with that, and besides your legal obligations you'll also need a bunch more systems to ensure your staff are performing well and servicing your clients consistently.

Here's some checklists to help guide you through the process.

Attracting applicants

- Create your staff member avatar.

- Write an advert that includes your mission. Use friendly language as well as the job details.

- Place your ad on Seek.

- Do a Facebook Live on your business page with the link to your Seek advert.

- Share the Live into relevant Facebook groups.

- Also boost the Live to massage therapists in your area in a 15-minute radius.

Be authentic with who you are as well as the type of person you want to attract. When you put yourself and your personality into the advert, it will click with the right kind of candidate.

Before they start

- Write a job description.

- Include their key performance indicators (KPIs) that will be used to measure their performance.

- Source a contract of employment – get help from an HR specialist with this as it's a legal document that must comply with legal requirements.

- Write a checklist of what you will teach and show them on day one.

The mechanics of employment are important as they form the foundation of your relationship with your team members, plus your business must comply with legal requirements.

The seamless onboard

The induction and training on a staff member's first day is a great beginning, then the next steps help to embed and confirm the environment and expectations while also continuing education. Schedule a series of catch-ups into your calendar for:

- first-day induction
- weekly staff meetings in the first four weeks
- monthly staff meetings after that
- quarterly one-on-one meetings to discuss KPIs.

CHAMPION SNAPSHOT: EILEEN EGERTON

Eileen from Nature's Formula massage has a wonderful way of engaging her staff and making sure things get done. Because we know that sometimes clients don't show up or forget or cancel at the last minute, she has a list of jobs that she has in categories for 5-minute jobs, 10-minute jobs, 15-minute jobs and 30-minute jobs. So if a client is going to be 10 minutes late the staff member can do a 10-minute job, and this gets documented in the jobs book so that jobs are not doubled up, and these are attached to their time sheet for greater accountability and transparency. This has helped to set up an amazing culture within her 20-plus team and across her three locations in Melbourne.

STAFF TASKS AND PROCEDURES

Once you've navigated the waters of taking on team members and have your team working with you, the next step is to have procedures for tasks they should be performing. These can include:

- *Cleaning list:* what jobs need to be done and when, including tasks that happen every three to six months, like cleaning air conditioner filters or dusting the ceiling fans.

- *Marketing:* like having a style guide for how you do your Facebook posting, when you launch adverts, writing a blog, how and when to send an email newsletter.

- *Finance:* how you record your expenses and payments; for example, using Xero, Quickbooks, or a simple spreadsheet.

- *Laundry:* where it gets washed and what day it gets delivered.

It will take time for your staff members to learn the ropes and get in the groove of your business, so be ready for that and make the transition as easy as possible by having clear procedures in place and even clearer expectations for performance.

OUTSOURCING

Every business has to do the core work it takes to produce their product or service – and this is something massage therapists rock at, using their skills to get great health outcomes. And you would realise by now that business owners also have to do admin, marketing, sales, and all the other jobs that are vital in order for this core service to be delivered through the business. "Chief cook and bottle washer" is how Elicia's grandpa puts it.

But as your business grows and you get busier with the activities of leadership and organisation, you should get someone else to do the low-value jobs – especially the ones you don't necessarily rock at – so that you can spend more time in the places your value is most important.

You can hire therapist staff, and in addition to treatments they will help with simple tasks like we mentioned earlier in this section, which will help. You can also get a receptionist to help with things in the office, like answering phones, making bookings, simple marketing, and doing data entry. And in other places in your business it is more appropriate to outsource to someone specific who has special skills in the right area or can do simple tasks at a lower cost to you.

The biggest trap that business owners fall into as they grow is getting into the habit of doing unimportant tasks themselves and not transitioning to getting help once it's the right time.

The second biggest trap is the complete opposite: people think, "I don't need to do that, I'll just get someone to do it for me", before they've mastered it themselves. The problem with this is that when you get someone to do something you don't understand or haven't mastered, you cannot guide what is needed or take responsibility for the results. We call this "abdicating", and it's a huge roadblock for some people.

So what's the difference between outsourcing and abdicating?

Outsourcing is leveraging your time in the most efficient way. You know the task that needs to be done and you can set the guidelines, expectations and outcomes. You can then pay someone to do the "grunt work" while you take the steps to fulfil your vision.

In this scenario you're still doing the required big-picture leadership and you're maintaining responsibility for the outcomes achieved.

This is the opposite to abdication, where you put responsibility into the hands of someone else and let them have control over areas of your business without knowing what they're doing or being empowered to guide results.

So we always recommend that you master every aspect of your business to a level of competence to allow you to lead someone else in that area. Then, when you are ready to outsource, think about getting someone to help with:

- laundry

- social media posts

- admin – answering phones, data entry

- bookkeeping – as you register for GST, or just get too busy to keep up by yourself

- website design, build or updates

- blog posts

- cleaning – in general, and especially things like windows.

For tasks like bookkeeping, you'll need a professional to help – and it's well worth it. Then, for many of these other areas you can think outside the square and may find that a simple post on a local community group on Facebook can get you someone amazing.

A great example is one way that we did this that saved us around $1000 per month at our clinic. We were getting charged a lot by our commercial laundry and they wouldn't negotiate on price. So we put a post on Facebook asking for someone to do our washing, which at that stage was around 150 towels per week with two drop-offs.

Within 24 hours, we had an application from a young mum with a baby. She was at home washing anyway and was happy to do the extra for the pay we negotiated. We had that lady for five or six months, then when she wanted to finish up we repeated the same post, and within 24 hours we found another mum who shared the job with her teenage daughter. They had a large family and were used to lots of washing; again, she came on board within 24 hours.

Both people we worked with fitted with our values and environment and appreciated the work we gave them, and were a significant saving compared to a commercial laundry.

Look at the tasks you do regularly and identify the ones that you can get help with. Do you need a professional to help with that? Or could you find someone in your local community who can fill the gap? Either way, find someone who aligns with your vision and can become part of your business team.

 ## USEFUL TOOL: VIRTUAL RECEPTION SERVICES

One of the simplest ways that small massage businesses lose bookings is when a potential client calls by phone to book and there's no-one to answer the phone. Not everyone will leave a message on voicemail, and even if they do the therapist needs to find a time to ring back and catch the caller before they book in somewhere else.

There is where outsourcing to someone like "Virtual Reception Services" can help. This company answers your phone for you and will book people in through your online booking system or take a message for you to return later. Some of our clients who use this service find they get extra bookings each week that would be lost otherwise.

RENTING A ROOM

Most therapists running their own business start small, working by themselves. Right now you might be working from a room at home, or doing just a couple of days for someone else in a clinic, or starting off doing mobile without any fixed location.

Sometimes people are happy to keep building their business like this, and if that's you then *rock on!* These are all legitimate business models, and if they match your goals then you can make any of these scenarios work. But if you are thinking of growing your business to beyond your four home walls, you will want an actual location to work from, so you will need to rent a space.

Before you do, sit down and look at some basic numbers. You worked out your breakeven point in chapter 10... what would that look like with the new rent included? How long could you survive on your current savings or loans, if you have zero new clients at the start?

If you know the numbers, you can negotiate if you need to – it never hurts to ask. For example, if you know your first six weeks will be difficult financially until you build up more clients into your new availability, you could ask for a reduced rent for the first four or six weeks.

If you are comfortable with your numbers, let's look at some of the ways you can make this work so that you can be more confident as you rent.

Renting a room (subleasing)

The most common way for someone to start out is to rent a room per day or week in another clinic, commonly in with other healthcare professionals like chiropractors or naturopathy. It's a great way to get a start in having your own space. It's short term with low commitment, which is less risky if things don't work out how you want. You may also learn a lot from working with other healthcare professionals, and there's the opportunity for cross-referrals, which can bring in new clients.

The main clinic owner will normally be the head lessee and have a commercial lease with the property owner (or they may be the actual property owner themselves). Then this main clinician will sublet rooms to other healthcare professionals like you, often per day.

Unfortunately, renting in this way isn't always very structured, and there are common practices in healthcare rentals that can get really grey. Let's look at some of the challenges when renting a room in a clinic set up like this.

You need to know what you stand for in business, and you need to find a values-matched place to work. Do the main clinic owner and other tenants share your values and philosophies? Will you be happy for your clients to see you aligned with these other businesses?

Then you want to see if the space is right; for example, does it have a floor that is suitable for dry needling? Or do you need a hand basin? What's the access like for your clients? The great thing is most of the time if it's already a clinic, these basics are already handled for you.

Once you have matched your values to theirs and you can see the place rocks, it's time to negotiate. What is their agreement? Is it in writing? How much is it and what does it include – just rent, or also laundry, reception, and HICAPS?

Clarity is key

A problem we see sometimes is that there will be a verbal agreement on how much is paid per day or week for the room, and then a bunch of other rules or agreements that are loosely talked about but may not be clearly defined. Some of the common scenarios that you need to clarify are:

- If the clinic takes a percentage of earnings instead of or in addition to rent, is there an upper cap? What if you decide to increase your hours? What if you sell products or run events?

- If it's a referral clinic, who owns your client list if you move on? Do you have constant access to the list so you can export it or market to them without asking permission?

- Does the clinic group have their own Facebook page and other marketing? How often will they promote you and who pays if you want to do an advert through that? Can you do that yourself?

- Who's responsible for marketing and getting new clients?

- Can you use their booking software? If you do, do you need to pay for it, and can you use it to market to your clients but not theirs?

You can certainly create a contract or agreement where these things are sorted out and work well – the biggest difficulties come when it's not clear or each party has different expectations. So never rent a room from a clinic without a written agreement in place.

Agree on the details you want to clarify. Then also think about what could be frustrating if and when you end up leaving for whatever reason down the track. For example, we had an osteo who rented a room from us; he used our booking software which was included in the rent that he paid us. When we scaled back the clinic at one point and moved, he was able to take his database and get his own software, which was fine. The problem was that we actually still had a copy of his client list in our software, and our new location was a room rented from a different osteo. Now, we act with

216

integrity and never shared his list with the new clinic owner – but we could have. And this example is why we always suggest that you have your own subscription for your booking software or database.

GETTING A COMMERCIAL SPACE

A commercial lease is a larger commitment where you rent a space – either a room or several rooms – directly from a landlord. You will get a commercial lease if you will be the only or main business at your location and plan to brand it with your own business name, put up signage and so on.

You may be familiar with residential leases from when you have rented your own home, but many things differ in a commercial lease. For starters, most commercial leases are longer, and automatically include an option to renew at the end of the term. They will often be known as 3×3×3 or 5×5×5 leases, which means you can rent them for three (or five) years and have the option to renew after the first three (or five) years, then you can have two more cycles. This brings stability to both you and the landlord.

Usually a commercial lease is for the space only, and it's up to you to fit it out at your own expense. If this is the case you'll need to add internal walls, finishings, furniture and so on. The landlord may also require you to pull everything out when you leave, so – although many are happy with leaving improvements to the property in place – you should budget for the possibility of having to take everything out again.

Also be aware that when you're working out your numbers for a commercial lease you'll need to factor in insurance, council rates, rubbish collection, water, cleaning, window washing, phone and internet, electricity, and any other property expenses.

So, in short, a commercial lease can be much more expensive but you've got much more control and stability. A commercial lease is an excellent option once your business is at the right stage. You can also negotiate terms, such as asking for the first one or two months rent free or discounted, or asking to have some of the fit-out covered by the landlord. Some of the insurances can be covered in your agreement. It's always worth asking, as any help you can get during this stage is a bonus to your bottom line.

HOW TO TRANSITION TO A NEW LOCATION

If you do decide to move from your current location, it's important to have a plan for the move, and for the finances you'll need in order to achieve it. It's a great idea to have a lot of momentum behind you with bookings as you go.

When OG Massage was growing there was a point when we moved from a single room into our own clinic. Before the move we built up our client numbers and staff to the point of being absolutely chock-a-block in the small space. We had five people treating out of one room, using split shifts. But it meant that when we moved to a clinic with three treatment rooms, we already had some momentum to carry us through.

CHAPTER 14

GROWTH PILLAR 2: RUN WORKSHOPS

Another really great way to leverage your time is by running workshops where you help multiple people in a room together. This is leveraged because each person is paying you but you're delivering your content to them all at once.

THREE AMAZING BENEFITS FOR YOUR BUSINESS

Running a successful workshop has three amazing benefits for your business.

Firstly, it's an excellent way to engage with your existing clients and cement your position as a Health Leader within your tribe. When you take responsibility for teaching or training someone in an area you are naturally seen as the leader (because you are).

It also means these existing clients are working with you more closely and learning from you outside of their treatments. By seeing you more often and aligning with your messages they are thinking about you and will naturally book in more often for treatment as well.

The second benefit to running workshops on health topics that are relevant to your community is that it attracts new people in. When you market your event to your local community you'll find some people will come along who have never been to see you before. A great tactic is to give each of these newbies a voucher to encourage them to come in for a treatment.

Thirdly, it's good for your reputation. This is true for people who are already clients and within your local broader community. People who come to your event see you at the front of the room leading and training people. This immediately frames you as a leader and raises your reputation. And even people who don't actually come to your events will still see your marketing and know that you're running them – and this in itself raises your profile in your community.

WHAT DOES A WORKSHOP LOOK LIKE?

A workshop is a class or training event. It usually involves teaching your audience or guiding them through an experience. Most commonly this is something like a 90-minute session held on a weeknight with anywhere from six to thirty attendees. It could be at your clinic if it's big enough, or at a local neighbourhood centre or similar.

Sometimes a workshop could also be a half-day or full day, or even a longer retreat-style event. These follow the same concept but are bigger, so they allow you to deliver more value and therefore charge more.

Some therapists run workshops on topics that they have received specific training in. For example, we see people who teach baby massage or couples massage because they themselves have received training on how to deliver these programs. This is awesome – a program that shows you how to present education like this usually provides you with a framework for the training, material you can reproduce and distribute, and sometimes you'll even get ideas about marketing the workshop too.

However, you don't need to have done special training to run a workshop for the general public. There are only two situations that you can't simply teach without a qualification or other special requirements: if you are delivering a government-certified course (like at a TAFE), or if you are teaching something that could cause injury or is considered "medical". So keep your workshops simple, fun and aimed at the public, and with topics that you are comfortable teaching to others.

This is also an opportunity to partner with another local Health Leader like a personal trainer or naturopath. By sharing the stage you can bring in extra expertise on an aligned topic, plus you get to advertise to each other's audiences so you can each be exposed to new people as potential clients.

HOW MUCH SHOULD I CHARGE?

The value you put on your event depends on your goals for it.

Some workshops are designed simply to build your reputation and encourage more people to book in for your treatments, so the workshop itself is not an income generator, it's a marketing activity. In this case you need to cover expenses but not much else, so a short evening workshop might be $5 or $10.

In other cases your workshops are true income pillars within your business, and if this is the case you need to charge accordingly. Do a mini-budget for your event to see all your expenses,

221

including marketing, venue hire, food and drinks. Then ensure you are earning enough to make it worth your time and energy. A half-day or full-day workshop will typically cost attendees somewhere between $150 and $800, and retreats over multiple days are $1000 to $5000, or even more as you build your reputation and create events that are even more special.

WHAT TOPIC SHOULD I CHOOSE?

A huge part of the success of your event will be the topic you choose. It must be powerful to get people interested enough to take action and commit to coming along. Some example topics include things like:

- posture for office workers

- better eating

- health and confidence for women

- living chemical-free

- essential oils

- couples massage

- introduction to Yoga or Pilates

- mobility as you age.

A great place to start is with a topic that you are already speaking with your clients about naturally. Chances are you're already repeating yourself several times a week with the same advice to different clients. Every time you catch yourself doing that you can note it to yourself as a potential workshop topic.

Think about it now: what topic would be a fit for you and your clients?

"Success isn't about how much money you make. It's about the difference you make in people's lives."

Michelle Obama

GAINING THE CONFIDENCE TO PRESENT

Some people are nervous about running a workshop because they feel that they lack the confidence to teach or lead other people in this way.

James tells a great story about teaching his very first class at TAFE. When he arrived at the class he didn't have a key yet so he waited outside the room with everyone else until a supervisor came to open up. He wasn't a whole lot older than most of the students, and it was a new year so most of them didn't know each other.

They all chatted for a few minutes, then as the group walked in James went to the front while everyone else went to their seats. One student audibly said to another, "Oh! I thought he was another student." The attitude in the room shifted and everyone spent the rest of the lesson learning from him as he stood out the front.

Do you see how this works? While they were outside, everyone chatted together and there was no difference between members of the group. But once they were inside, the act of behaving like a teacher made James a teacher within the group. When you are at the front of the room at your own workshop, everyone will be ready to experience you the same way. They are not there to judge, and if they're not interested in the topic they would have stayed at home.

Behave like the leader in the room and everyone will slip into their role as learners. And before long you'll have practised this enough that it will become natural.

CREATING AN EXPERIENCE

You want your workshop to be both memorable and life-changing for the people in the room. In order to create this level of impact your workshop should be an immersive experience, not just a lecture. There are many different ways to make this happen depending on your topic and skill set. An example outline for a 90-minute session could include:

- A time for casual chatting at the start, ideally with tea and coffee.

- An interactive component at the beginning, like an exploratory Q&A or five minutes of "say hi to the person next to you".

- Your introduction, connecting the topic with the audience and building you as an authority to show why this topic is important and why you've invited them today.

- The theory behind what it is that you're delivering.

- A practical exercise for people to do, which they can participate in during the event (it's even better if they can get feedback).

- A look at how this replaces or fits around their old patterns.

- A Q&A for people to ask specific questions or get help.

Different people learn in different ways, so you need to have components of different learning styles throughout the event, so that everyone has the opportunity to connect with you and your topic in their own way. If you're doing a longer workshop or a multi-day retreat you'll need to include more experiential sessions, and your topic will guide you.

FILLING THE ROOM

There are two types of workshop attendees: existing clients and new people. Luckily the basic strategy you will use to fill your workshop room is the same for both groups.

Remember that workshops are a pillar within your existing business, they do not stand separately. So it needs to feel to your tribe that your event is aligned with everything else you are doing. When they see it coming up they should think, "Yes, of course, that makes total sense".

One way of creating this alignment is to use your content marketing. Eight weeks before your event you can write a blog post or create a video on the topic you plan to run your event on. Then you post about it on social media regularly for a week or two before doing a second blog post or video on a related theme and continuing the social posts.

You should also use email, SMS or Facebook chat to send a message out to your existing clients with a link to the content.

All the buzz at this point is being built around the content itself – no-one even knows you're running an event yet. This is "priming the pump". You can gauge the level of interest your audience has and this can guide you to adjust your plans for the event topic if needed. They should be excited enough by the content that they are commenting or messaging you. This gives you a measure of how successful the topic will be for a workshop, and also builds awareness and interest in what you do.

A week after your second major content piece the buzz is in full swing, and this is when you announce the details of your event and start accepting signups. Have an early bird offer to encourage early registrations for those who can commit.

With this level of forward planning and opportunity for feedback you are raising awareness and testing your audience's need level before doing the majority of the planning and creating required for the event itself. This saves time and effort while making sure you have people lined up to attend the event when it's released.

You will also do all your normal marketing as well of course, and put photos from the event itself all over social media. You can also have the event videoed and use edited snippets of your presentation as fantastic content for social media in the future. Use everything you can from the event to your advantage.

NEXT STEPS

People are the most engaged with you that they will ever be when they are at a live event and it's going well. There's a fabulous energy in the room and lives are being changed, whether on a small or large scale. Many people will want to connect with you even more so they can feel this excitement again and have another experience like this, so you should always have the next steps available for them at the event.

In some cases the next step will be to book in for a treatment with you one on one. In other cases you will be offering a larger event; for example, a half-day workshop might lead into a three-day retreat that expands on the same topics and takes it to the next level.

Whatever your next step is, be prepared with a special offer at your workshop so that the people who are ready and motivated can buy in immediately.

CHAPTER 15

GROWTH PILLAR 3: SELL A PRODUCT

Selling a product is another core Growth Pillar you can choose to build in your business in order to make it more stable and secure. Selling products as a pillar means more than just stocking spiky balls or heat bags. Those kinds of products are great to help raise the average dollar spend and get better outcomes for clients. But while selling products from your desk at checkout is a completely awesome thing to do, it's simply part of your massage practice. The new pillars you build as you grow need to be more powerful than that so they can bring extra income and stability to your business. When we talk about product as a Growth Pillar, we mean using a specific brand that will bring people in and get sales *in addition* to the times they come in for treatment.

If your practice incorporates beauty treatments then you might be doing this already – salons are great at using and stocking "salon only" brands that encourage clients to return to buy more when they run out. Another option is to produce your own unique brand of products by working with a manufacturing company. This enables you to use them yourself, and even to sell them through other businesses or online if you want to.

But a more common route for supplying products is to join a network marketing company, also known as a multi-level marketing company (MLM), and that's what we're going to focus on here.

MULTI-LEVEL MARKETING

The idea is that an MLM company can supply you a product range (different companies supply different things) and you get a commission on sales you make. Plus, a core concept in MLM is that you can sign other people up so they also get wholesale prices – and you still get a small commission on their ongoing purchases. In this way it helps to build extra income beyond what normal product sales can.

Now let us point out quickly that we're not here to try to convince you to do network marketing if you don't want to, nor is it something we think is essential to run a successful business. Some people like it, others don't do it on principle! If you've had bad experiences in the past and don't want to go there again then we're not here to change your mind… there are three other Growth Pillars you can use if this isn't your cup of tea. However, many massage therapists find that the right network marketing company aligns with their goals for their community impact and their business growth and provides a product and a structure to help meet both.

MLM myths and fears

Let's start by looking at some of the common myths and fears around MLM companies, as well as the legitimate problems you need to look out for.

The way we see it, MLM is just a business structure products. But as a concept it's got a poor reputation with ple. In our Massage Business Support Network online other topic as controversial as MLM! It brings out strong opinions on both sides.

By far the biggest issue MLM has as a concept is that so many people have been burnt by being on the receiving end of absolutely terrible tactics by someone new to network marketing. Almost all of the negativity people can have around it comes down to either a bad experience they've had with a specific company, or a bad experience with someone in a company trying to do a "hard sell". Have you ever received one of those messages on Facebook from a friend you barely know that says, "I'd like to talk to you about an opportunity. I can't say what it is but I'd like to meet!" Both of us still get these messages or similar regularly, and it drives us crazy. Honestly, who is going to respond to something like that? Or recently, James was contacted by someone he did a course with a couple of years ago, who was in town and wanted to catch up for a coffee. James went to meet him at a café thinking he was rekindling a friendship, when five minutes in the guy pitched a new MLM program he'd just signed up to. Yuck!

These kinds of tactics leave a bad taste in the mouth, and rightly so – they use misleading messages and try to leverage a relationship to make sales.

We *never* recommend this kind of selling.

For businesspeople like you, if you do MLM it will be as part of your existing business. You already have a client base that is used to buying from you, so this is simply another way to meet their needs. Your clients can expect you to recommend products (and other services) that are going to be beneficial to them, and of course they can choose to buy them or not – just the same as with anything else you recommend. In this case the product happens to be an MLM product, and as long as you believe it's beneficial you can truly and wholeheartedly recommend it. You can even offer for clients to join themselves if they want to… if they do experience benefits from the product then why wouldn't they want to get them cheaper? But you won't be pushing them into it. There's no hard sell, no friendships being damaged, and you're only supplying products that you know will help people.

The legitimate problems that can happen with MLM are similar to any product supplier.

You need to be absolutely sure that the product you're selling does what it says it will do, and that you are recommending it to your clients because it will help them. The big MLMs in the health and wellness industry tend to be pretty good, but there are plenty of smaller companies that make promises they can't keep, so do some research and make sure you've tried the products yourself before recommending them.

A related issue with MLM is the way sales and trailing income are tied to the company itself. If you're very closely connected with an MLM and you've built up the trailing commissions to give you a reasonable income from it, that's great. But you must be sure the company is solid. It takes a lot of work for you to get to that level, and if it's a smaller company that changes or goes out of business it can leave you high and dry.

So do your research, talk with other people who are already working with the MLM, use the products yourself, and always be honest in your recommendations to clients. This is the only way MLM products should be included in your business.

"It is our choices that show what we truly are, far more than our abilities."

J. K. Rowling

Product benefits

The first benefits you should be looking for in any product you sell are the benefits to your clients. Any product you recommend must align with the health goals you have for them. So usually that means choosing one of the many companies that supplies health products, essential oils, supplements, or something else that fits.

Some popular companies that we see massage therapists working with at the moment are:

- doTerra or Young Living for essential oils

- Herbalife, Isagenix or Juice Plus for health supplements.

The other benefit to MLM is how the products fit into your business ecosystem and add to your bottom line. Using an MLM for products has a few great business benefits:

- access to a range of products (depending which supplier you choose)

- the products are not usually available to the public at retail outlets, so your clients can't buy them off the shelf somewhere else

- there are options to sign up other members, which brings trailing commissions and income over time.

The exact commission structure is different for each company, but the trailing commission for signing up other members is where the focus often is.

There's no such thing as truly "passive" income – everything that generates cashflow requires you to give people value and do something (and if it doesn't need your input then it's not something a Health Leader should be involved in). But the trailing commissions on MLM signups are a perfect example of "leveraged" income, which is the purpose of the Growth Pillars. You make an income from these commissions that leverages the time and effort you put into it.

For you, as a Health Leader and existing business owner, you can choose to engage with MLM at any level you want. Some people do choose to take it quite seriously and put great time and energy into building their network so that they can create a leveraged income to replace or exceed what they get from the rest of their business. More likely, you'll want to create this in conjunction with your other pillars, meaning you'll build it over time to give you a good income balanced with the leverage you create in other places.

THE POWER CIRCLE

To be as powerful as possible as a pillar in your business, your chosen MLM needs to be integrated into the other parts of what you do. You're not building separate businesses here, it should fold together into a cohesive whole.

A great way of doing this is to use what we call the "Power Circle", which combines your MLM product sales with your workshops and your treatments. When it's set up right, each of the three parts of the Power Circle feeds the others. This results in better client retention and engagement, and more powerful outcomes in their lives.

The strategy is quite simple:

1   You have regular clients who come in for treatments. Your products are for sale in your clinic over the counter to the people who come in.

2   You run a short workshop or class on a health topic that will align with your audience and the services you provide.

The workshop is advertised to existing clients as well as new people.

3 At the workshop, attendees can buy the products at retail price, or sign up for the MLM company if they want to. All attendees are also given a special bonus voucher to come in for a treatment, which helps them convert to clinic clients if they haven't been in before.

Can you see how this works? Each part of the strategy supports the other parts, so your clients are encouraged to be more connected with you at each step, and the marketing you do for any one part of the Power Circle will ultimately benefit every part of your business.

When you can see the power and simplicity of this we would encourage you to look at your own business with an open mind. Is there a place for MLM products among your Growth Pillars?

CHAMPION SNAPSHOT: JASON BROOKER

Jason is a massage therapist who introduced doTerra essential oils as a product by using them in treatments and then selling them to clients at the checkout. He also sold some of the oils at a local market, and it was so popular that he realised he could run workshops specifically about the oils and use that to gain new clients. With regular workshops the oil sales took off and he began signing other people up to the company when they were interested, and over time this side of his business grew to a point where this income matched what he was making from doing 15 to 20 treatments each week, all while staying aligned to his mission of improving the health of his clients.

CHAPTER 16

GROWTH PILLAR 4:
CREATE A PROGRAM

The final Growth Pillar we'll look at is creating a program. This is one of the most powerful pillars if you want to grow your reputation even larger and wider as a Health Leader.

GOING GLOBAL

A digital program is a way to guide your clients through learning and experiences using educational tools like video, workbooks and feedback. And you can present your program entirely online, so that it can be delivered to anyone in the world. This ability to work with anyone means you can make a real impact in your chosen niche and break free from the geographic limitations that the other Growth Pillars have.

Online programs are common among Health Leaders who grow a reputation too big to be able to handle clients one on one. Think of people like Michelle Bridges, the personal trainer who was on

237

TV on *The Biggest Loser*. We bet it costs a bomb to get a one-on-one session with Michelle… but luckily her online program gives you her best material for a much better price.

You don't have to be on TV to make an online program work for you, but Michelle is a great example of someone who has moved up the ladder and is now able to leverage her time enormously well. For you, as part of your business, the program pillar is quite a flexible pillar. Your program can be small or large, cheap or high value, short or long. What you choose to do will depend on where you are currently on the Health Leader Ladder, what your goals are, and the journey you want to take your clients on.

CHAMPION SNAPSHOT: KRISTY RACKHAM

Kristy is a single mum homeschooling her two kids, one with special needs. When we met Kristy she was only doing a handful of massage treatments each month because she found it took too much time away from her other commitments. Instead, she used her skills as a Registered Nurse and holistic practitioner to create an online program that helps people to overcome anxiety without medication. It's still been a challenge fitting this in around her busy lifestyle, but creating and delivering this program allows better flexibility in hours and a much more leveraged income. Plus Kristy gets to help people all over Australia!

Creating your own program has a lot of excellent advantages for your business. But it also comes with new challenges. It's not easy to create a program from scratch if you've never done it before. It's a very different process from being a solo therapist, and it requires a good deal of commitment to make it happen successfully. (By the way, it's definitely worth it.)

What we're going to give you here is an overview of the style of program we help our more advanced therapists and Health Leaders create, so you can see the concept of how it works and you can brainstorm what this will look like if you choose to make it part of your journey. This will give you a good place to start, and we'll also point you in the right direction about where you can learn the rest of what you need to when you get to this level.

Just like with the other pillars, there's nothing saying you must create a program. But when it's done right it's a powerful way to scale.

WINNING PROGRAM COMPONENTS

The purpose of your online program is to create a result in your client's life. Whatever this looks like for you, the program needs to be structured in a way that enables it to happen the best.

The first part of any program creation is to nail the outcome you want to create in your clients and then mind map everything you know that could help them. Do a huge brain dump; write everything down and join it all with lines and scribble and colour and anything else that's meaningful. This is a time to be creative! It's better to put a lot down and then cut some of it out later – so get scribbling!

Once you've got all that knowledge and experience out of your head, you can organise it into categories; see what fits and what needs to be removed, and how it will break down into sections or modules within your program.

Once you've got that, you can neaten it up into a list of what you'll teach in each module, and these modules each become a day or week in your program. You can organise the content by topic instead of time if you choose, so that people who join can access everything they need to. However, in our experience it often works better to lead people through the content in a logical order so it's really clear exactly what to do and when.

Almost every successful program has three major aspects that enable outcomes to happen:

- structured learning
- community engagement
- feedback and help.

People learn in different ways, so having these various parts to your program delivered differently means that as a whole your program is catering to a broader range of learning styles. Your structured learning is usually delivered on a website portal and will involve videos, written information and practical exercises for people to do. Community engagement can happen through a private clients-only Facebook group. And feedback and individual help can be handled using live webinar training or one-on-one phone calls.

CHOOSING A PROGRAM TOPIC AND LENGTH

It's similar to a workshop in the way topics are chosen – you need something that connects with your audience and which you can teach in a way that will get results for your clients.

A program can be something quite small and easy that adds value for your existing clients. Think of small programs that might benefit people in between clinic visits; for example, "Better posture for office workers" or "7-day introduction to mindfulness". These might be priced anywhere from $49 to $295 and become primarily an upsell or cross-sell for existing clients.

Even a small program can help grow your reputation locally if you put it out there to the right people, and that can attract new clients to your clinic. Another cool benefit of a small program like this is that you can bundle it with massage treatments and reduce the overall cost without needing to discount your time, because an online program doesn't take any time to deliver once it's been set up. For example, "Buy a bundle of 5 treatments and get access to our special 3-day relaxation program free, normally worth $95!"

Small programs like this can be a fun way to dip your toes into online training. You can experiment to see what topics work for your audience, and they're quicker and easier to create so there's less risk if it doesn't work out the way you imagine.

However, if you want a program to become a major pillar in your business and grow beyond your current client base you must create a premium program that is $1000 or more. At this level you should be thinking of a 6- to 12-week program that delivers powerful change or solves an important problem for participants. Charging a reasonable amount for a program like this means you have the resources available to do marketing and sales for it and still value your time and expertise. By charging more you can work with fewer clients, and this lets you create a bigger transformation for them by giving them more time and energy.

OVERCOMING YOUR FEARS ABOUT RUNNING A PROGRAM

Even when therapists can see the benefits of creating an online program and can see other people doing it successfully, there are two major fears that can get in the way:

- Often therapists feel unworthy or feel they are not confident enough to create training on a topic.

- Therapists often say they don't know where to start with the tech side of things.

Let's consider each of these.

Gaining the confidence to run a program

Firstly, let's get this clear. You already know way more than your average client does. Most therapists do at least a couple of years of study, plus professional development after that, plus have hands-on experience treating people – sometimes hundreds of clients each year. This gives you massive insight into problems that you deal with regularly, and you will no doubt have developed your own ways to treat problems and connect with clients.

It's easy to undervalue how much this training and experience is worth to others when you're in the middle of it every day. But you have an amazing store of knowledge and wisdom just waiting to be shared with the average person who comes to see you. This is the point to creating a program: to distil the experience and knowledge you already have into something actionable that will get an outcome for the clients who join. You're already making changes in your clients' lives when they come to see you, this is just putting that knowledge online so you can impact more people.

Having fun with technology

There's a few areas of technology you're going to need to be aware of to create a program.

Recording video

Firstly, you'll need to record the videos. Don't be too concerned with the hardware right now, but take a look at the section opposite for details of what we use and recommend.

There are basically three types of videos you'll use:

1 Face-to-camera, where you deliver training by recording yourself speaking into the camera.

2 "How-to" videos; for example, if you're showing how to stretch or meditate.

3 Slideshows, where you record your voice over a slide presentation. This is useful for delivering factual information.

For the first two video types you'll use a video camera to record them, and the third type uses software on your computer to record the slides on screen as you speak.

No matter which style of video you're using for any given module, you should lead people through your content in a structured way that gives people an experience of what you do as well as the information itself. It's worth doing some basic training on presentation skills if you haven't already got experience in this area, so that you can communicate your concepts as clearly as possible.

USEFUL TOOL: VIDEO EQUIPMENT

For a high-value program you should use something better than a standard mobile phone. Many semi-pro SLR cameras record excellent video when paired with a plug-in microphone.

This is the setup we use for all our face-to-camera training:

- Canon EOS 700D (digital SLR) camera

- Rode wireless lapel microphone

- tripod

- two large softbox lights (ordered from eBay).

Most professionals would consider this "amateur" or "entry level" equipment, but it's a step up from a mobile phone and gives plenty of flexibility with what you want to record. Of course, you can shoot on whatever you have, or buy fancier equipment if you want to, but try to get the balance between quality and affordability so that you can make a start as soon as possible.

Creating the training portal

The other major technology you'll need is the web training portal you'll use to deliver your program. This happens through a website login so that you can give each of your clients access to your program.

You can create your own training portal using WordPress and one of the many plugins available for creating member training portals. Our favourite plugin is OptimizeMember because of the marketing tools it comes with, and other popular choices include MemberPress and LearnDash.

To go down this path you'll need to have a WordPress website up and running and be comfortable installing plugins and creating your module pages. All of the packages we've mentioned above have plenty of training videos and support, so if you've done any web editing before you should be able to learn what you need to in order to set this up.

If this all sounds like too much messing about then another option is to use an online training platform that is already set up for creating portals exactly like this. A training platform will usually cost a little more but they're generally easier to use because all your page templates and structure are ready to go and you can simply create your content and put it in. You'll still need to do some editing but it's a much easier process. Options for training and membership platforms like this include New Kajabi, Thinkific and ClickFunnels. They all have different strengths and weaknesses, so try them out to find the one that suits you and your program the best.

Of course, if you already have a web company that manages your site, they should be able to help you set up your training program. Or, if you don't have a web team but you really don't want to take on the tech side of things yourself, you can do your homework to find a reputable company and pay them to set up your platform. It will still require a lot of input from you, but you won't have to worry about the technical details.

Whichever way you go, creating your membership portal is going to be technically the trickiest part of setting up your program. But the thing is, it's not the most valuable. Your content is the most important part of what you are doing, so think of the portal as simply a necessary step in getting your membership content out to the people who need it.

ATTRACTING HIGH-VALUE CLIENTS TO YOUR PROGRAM

Getting people into your high-value program is a strategic process that might look quite different from what you've done to build the other parts of your business. You need to find the right people for your program – people who will benefit from what you are offering, achieve good results, and be happy to pay for the outcomes they get. Some of your existing clients from your hands-on practice may be suitable, but you'll also be promoting this program to new audiences.

The sales funnel for your program

The great thing about a high-value program is that with each new sale you will get the funds to pay for more advertising and marketing, so the more it grows the better your budget gets. In most cases you'll create a more sophisticated marketing and sales funnel for your program, because it is a bigger decision for your clients because of the time commitment and the higher price point. Your goal is to attract the right kind of clients with your marketing so that when you speak to them for a signup call you're only speaking to people who are ready to go.

To attract the right people you should start with great content. Create articles or blog posts containing simple and brilliant advice or education, then share them through social media. People who are interested in these topics are naturally the right fit for your program, so as they read or watch they are becoming familiar with who you are and what you stand for. This is the same "content marketing" strategy we looked at earlier for the massage side of your business, but you will do it here to attract your new ideal clients for your program.

Rather than do direct sales advertising like what is most common for the massage side of your business, instead you will create what we call a "lead magnet" or "hook" to offer as the next step through your marketing funnel. This is essentially a valuable piece of flagship content on a topic that your tribe are highly motivated about. In order to get this piece of information, people need to give you their name and email, and sometimes phone number, in exchange. I'm sure you've seen these lead magnets online – if you haven't you can sign up for one of ours on www.massagechampions. com ;)

You promote your lead magnet through Facebook ads or other top-of-funnel activity, and when people enter their details you can call them to touch base and see if they are a right fit for your program.

An ongoing email sequence can be automated so that anyone who signs up gets a couple of emails each week for a few weeks that also gives them loads of value with advice and content, and includes more offers to join your program.

There are a number of variations on the types of campaigns you can run, and many options for the way your content and lead magnets are presented. Imagine live webinars, ebooks, video trainings, and in-person events used for promotion. You might do some of these or all of them... it's your choice. The only rule is – don't stop creating until you find what works. And even then, what works for you right now might not work for more than a few months, so you will always be experimenting with new ideas and seeing what connects best with your audience.

If this sounds more sophisticated than what you've done before for marketing, that's because it is! Multi-step campaigns like this are part of the standard online marketing toolkit but are rarely needed for local business marketing, which is why you won't normally use them for promoting your main massage services. Marketing a high-value program is a strategic process that you need to experiment with in order to move into the higher rungs of the ladder, and it's a step above the learning you will have done before.

But just like anything else you've learned on your journey, if you are ready to commit the time and energy to making a program work you will take it step by step and it will get done. You'll learn what you need to, make mistakes, stand up again and keep climbing the ladder.

The end point on this journey is where you choose it to be.

ARE YOU READY TO GROW?

If you're currently a solo therapist the Growth Pillars may seem exciting to you – or maybe a little intimidating. Even if you're already a few rungs up the ladder, running a team or providing leveraged services, you'll find the rungs above you can look even higher and scarier the closer you get to them.

That's okay! Because it takes time to grow into these places.

If you think the person you are right now couldn't handle running a business like that – you're right. But by the time you are at the higher level rungs on the ladder, you'll also have learnt a lot and fundamentally changed some of the ways you think about yourself (remember how important your mindset is). The person you are right now is designed to handle the business you have right now. When you have overcome your current challenges and learnt what you need to, that's when you get to upgrade to new levels of challenge.

By the time you're two or three rungs higher up the ladder you have changed who you are so that you can handle your business at that level. Then you can choose to stay comfortable at that level or keep learning and growing. Your business is your ultimate personal development tool. In practical terms, this means that right now you only need to focus on the rung you are at in the ladder right now, and the next one above it. The tasks you have in front of you right now are going to give you the practical and personal skills you need to master that, and then keep moving up if you choose to.

CHAPTER 17

THE SEVEN TRUTHS BEHIND RUNNING A SUCCESSFUL MASSAGE BUSINESS

We love massage therapists.

Massage and related therapies are changing the health of the world. More than ever before, healthy touch is commonly not a part of the daily experience for most people. Stress and anxiety are at a high. Postural conditions are increasing due to work and technology habits.

But massage changes everything.

As a therapist you are a champion of loving kindness who is part of the most "touchy-feely" revolution the world has ever seen. You are creating health and healing using intuition and connection as much as the art of physical therapy, in a way that is accessible to everyone, at any age. And that's why it's vital that massage therapists build great businesses. Because this is too important to ignore, and this industry must rise to prominence so that more people can be impacted by what happens on the massage table.

Most massage therapists start with a passion to help others. Maybe you did too. And you want to be successful. You want to help even more clients. And you want to be able to look back and say… *YES! I did that!* But when it comes to the business side of things … let's just say that until now… maybe… "it's not a strength". Even after reading this book, perhaps you're thinking, "I'll try a few of these things", but you might not be ready to go all out and dedicate as much passion to supporting your practice as to your technique.

IT'S UP TO YOU

Now, this part is important… so listen up.

Right now we want to deliver what is going to be the most important message you will hear on your journey to being a truly successful therapist, business owner and Health Leader in your community. We know it's often a challenge for therapists to think of themselves as Health Leaders who will accept the challenges of business in order to achieve their goals. But it's time to hear the truth. In fact, we've broken it down into seven truths that you need to know in order to be successful as a massage therapist. And the reason this is so profound is that these truths make up the biggest difference between people who struggle to turn massage into a career and those who succeed.

The tough thing for us is seeing both ends of the spectrum. We speak with hundreds of therapists every year, and we get to see what it looks like to be in major struggle town year after year, right through to the people who are doing six figures and beyond as they succeed in massage. So many people are amazing at what they do and *deserve* to be fully booked. But they're not.

The fact is that moving up the Health Leader Ladder is challenging. It takes skills that are very different to therapy itself. But the challenges must be overcome if you as an individual are to succeed long term as a therapist and if massage as a profession is to flourish. So now we are going to share the seven truths about running a successful massage business that most therapists are not aware of or don't want to face. If you master these, you will be on the road to success.

It's up to you.

Truth #1: You must be good at marketing

You must become good at marketing and overcome the fear of "getting out there".

The "build it and they will come" idea that so many of the old guard in the profession still teach simply doesn't work in today's world. It's slow, uncontrolled and passive. Yet we ran a survey of over 500 therapists and found that the vast majority report they only do between zero and five marketing campaigns a year. These are also the same people that don't have the number of clients they'd like to. They are relying on "build it and they will come" – and it's not working.

Proactive marketing is the only way to build your business and see more clients.

Truth #2: You must be comfortable with sales

You must be comfortable with sales – with setting the right price point, booking clients in, rebooking them, and with selling products.

Sales is just connecting someone who has a need with a person who can meet that need – you. Hesitation in sales only ever means that you don't believe in the product at some level. So if you're hesitant selling yourself it means you don't value yourself highly enough.

Trust yourself! Believe in yourself! Once you have confidence in yourself and your outcomes, sales will be easy. And nothing works in business without it.

Truth #3: You must know your numbers

You must see and understand the important numbers in your business, and at least be able to tell what your breakeven point is, how many treatments you need to perform each week to pay for all your expenses, and how much profit you make after that on each treatment.

Numbers can be easy if you make them easy – way easier than all the muscle group origins and insertions that you already have memorised. So put the time and effort in that you need in order to make your numbers work. Without them you're just making decisions based on guesswork.

Truth #4: You must invest in training and your business

Starting a massage business is relatively inexpensive compared to many other types of business. After your own training investment, equipment and startup costs are very low.

However, some therapists still have an aversion to spending anything at all. They only want to do free marketing and resent investing anything at all to improve their business or themselves. Every business needs money to flourish. When you spend, treat it as an investment that will bring you a massive return if you spend in the right places.

"It takes courage to grow up and become who you really are."

E. E. Cummings

Be comfortable with spending money to grow your business. It's vital, so just plan it out, put it in your budget and work through it.

Truth #5: You must not make excuses

The biggest roadblock that will slow you down on your way to reaching your goal is the stories you tell yourself about why you can't do it. To become a Health Leader and successful business owner you must be responsible for your own behaviour. You must live from cause.

Excuses come in all forms; we often hear things like, "I can't charge more in my area", "I don't have enough time for that", "I don't have enough money to pay for advertising", or, "I'm not qualified enough". The thing is, we've heard all these excuses – and we have also seen people who were in a way worse position tell themselves a different story, take action to make things happen, and achieve great success.

We have clients who started in massive debt, who are single mums with four kids, and who have moved to new towns and don't know anybody. And even though it's really difficult, these people make it work. And you can too, if you choose to.

Truth #6: You must not let others limit your thinking or behaviour

As therapists it's a natural gift to spend time in your treatments making people feel comfortable.

But problems happen when you take that attitude into the rest of your life. Your Mum or Dad, your siblings, your friends, and even other therapists might say, "Are you *still* doing that?" or, "Why did you put another ad out on Facebook? You know people hate advertising." The thing is, these people are bringing you into line with their own expectations, and it's a natural response to want to make these people feel comfortable.

But reinforcing their attitude is not what is actually best for them – and it's certainly not what is best for you. Break free from their outlook on life, and make the people with limiting beliefs feel uncomfortable!

Truth #7: You must commit

You are a Health Leader and a champion to your clients and community. If you take that vision seriously then it is your duty and responsibility to overcome your fears and succeed in business so that you can help and lead more clients.

When you are seeing more clients you will be improving the health of more people – you also receive more abundance yourself, so your clients benefit, you benefit, your family benefits – plus, success itself has huge positive energy that revitalises the community around you and allows you to spread your message wider and wider. Being a Health Leader also means owning your space as a business leader and doing whatever needs to be done in business to make that happen.

So our message to you is that you are in control of this, and we're going to explain why. These seven truths serve to highlight what therapists are most afraid of. You can use the enemy of fear to overcome them.

And the enemy of fear is *commitment*.

For example, we know when we started we were certainly afraid of many of these truths simply because we didn't know any better. We remember when James was running his agency and helping Elicia at the clinic as well, and within the space of two years he signed up for a professional development program and a business coach, and Elicia entered a coaching program to help her along too.

In that two years we committed to over $45,000 of coaching and development. We had fears about that, of course... our combined incomes had been only marginally more than that amount in the year previous! So, we were trusting on change to happen in order to meet our obligations. We had our family counting on us, our clients counting on us, we were in the process of buying our first home, and we were denied getting an extension on our overdraft with the bank.

It was stressful – but we made it work.

The commitment of our time and money was a signal to ourselves that we were stepping up, that we were committing to the vision that we had for our clients, and stepping up into our calling. And we have never looked back – even when times were tough and we didn't know exactly what to do next, the commitment we placed on ourselves drove us forward.

Now the problem we see with most massage therapists and myotherapists is that they know they want to commit to their end goals and they know what it looks like for them to have their perfect career in this industry. But when it comes to taking action towards it and doing the steps along the way, they find the fear traps them and stops them from moving forward. The fear of the large and small tasks, marketing, numbers, sales, investing money, putting themselves out there – it keeps them from achieving their big goals.

Small fears can hold you back from big achievements. Instead, what would it be like to truly be a Health Leader? To know that you're taking the right course of action for yourself and building a healthy business that is encouraging others in their health too?

Are you ready to make a truly successful career out of massage?

Are you ready to be that Health Leader?

Because if you are, it's time to commit.

Truly **COMMIT**.

Put yourself out there. Do what it takes.

Make a decision – and then take action. And then do it again. And again. And again.

Decide 100% that this is who you are – and *boom*. *GAME OVER*.

You *win*. Your family *wins*. Your clients *win*. The hundreds – or even thousands – of others in your community who will be impacted by your positivity and proactivity will *win*.

You've got this. We know you do. We believe in you. We are proud of you.

Put fear to the side, commit, and take action. Now. Today. Because you've got so much riding on you, now and in your future. So step up, own your amazing potential. Back yourself. Trust yourself. Honour this journey and be proud to rise to the challenge and create a rocking business.

You've got this.

You are a massage champion.

James and Elicia Crook

ACKNOWLEDGEMENTS

We recognise that we have learned so much from our mentors and thought leaders, both in the training and knowledge they've provided and in their guidance and support as we've navigated our own business challenges. There have been many tearful learnings and deep breakthroughs on our path, and we are eternally grateful to God for all the special people we've met along the journey so far and for the powerful influence they have had on our lives.

Special acknowledgement must go to:

Andrew Griffiths, for first lighting the spark of a book in us.

Ryan Madgiarz, for being an energetic inspiration and challenging us to think bigger.

Matthew Church, for guiding us with wisdom through difficult changes.

Taki Moore, for being a role model business leader and family man.

Joanne Clark, for taking us deeper into understanding ourselves and other humans.

Zachary Dixon, for showing us the power of heart-centred honesty.

Sarah Valentine, for coaching us in our first businesses so many years ago.

And to our very special coaching friends who always inspire us to be the best version of ourselves, who hold the space and call us on our BS ... and love us through the process: Louise, Karen, Mary, Natta, David, John and Erin, Annette, and Mike. Thank you!

And to our staff and clients, past and present. We love you all.

Also the inspirational thought leaders and trainers who have led the way with their innovation and generous education. We learn from so many people but these deserve a special mention:

Russell Brunson
Brené Brown
Gary Vaynerchuk
Amy Porterfield
Jim Collins
Ryan Deiss
Simon Sinek
Alison Armstrong
Mark Driscoll

You should check them out too.

Elicia Crook and James Crook present...

MASSAGE CHAMPIONS
Business Coaching For Massage Therapists

We help passionate Massage Therapists see
25 clients per week consistently, and become
Fully Booked Without Burnout.

We also show Business Owners and those ready to take
the next steps how to create multiple growth pillars and
reach a sustainable 6 Figure income from massage.

*Change lives, impact the world, and turn your
passion into a rocking business.*

**Join our FREE "Massage Business Support Network"
on Facebook for free trainings and inspiration!**

READER BONUS

**Do you want help implementing a strategy
from this book? Or have a question about
how to move to your next step?**

For a FREE 15-minute clarity call, book in at:

massagechampions.com/reader

CPSIA information can be obtained
at www.ICGtesting.com
Printed in the USA
LVHW012234210820
663785LV00005B/211

9 780994 328427